ZOOM IN ON

THE HUMAN BODY

ADAPTED BY

SALLY MORGAN

KINGFISHER

Contents

A Story

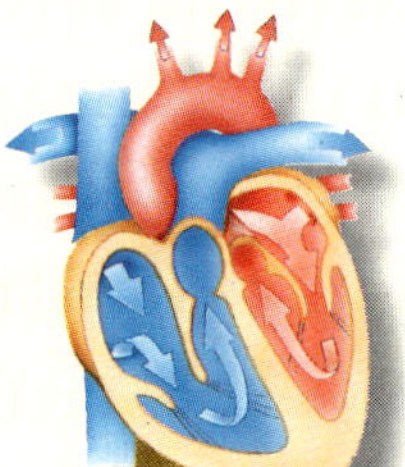

Information

An Activity

Information

A Game

Information

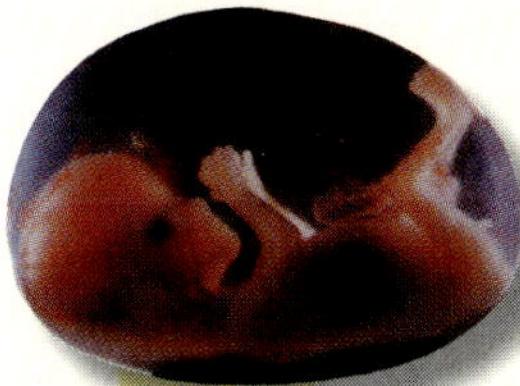

Stickers

Postcards

A Pen-friend across the Sea

Crossing the estuary

As it rang out, the boat's siren startled into flight a colony of seagulls that had gathered on the upper deck. Resting his elbows on the ship's rail, Gregory watched them scatter into the sky and wheel around the lighthouse at the entrance to the harbour of Brick City. In spite of the spray carried by the strong wind, he had spent the entire crossing up on deck, because he did not want to miss a single moment of this expedition. Expedition? It was scarcely an hour's voyage between the two banks of the estuary. But the word was no exaggeration. It was the first time Gregory had left Glassborough all by himself. For him, this crossing was a real adventure, even if he was going to spend only two days at the home of Barbara Griffon, his pen-friend.

As agreed, Barbara and her father were waiting for him under the sign 'Travellers Exit'. Thanks to three or four photos she had slipped into her many letters, Gregory recognized his pen-friend immediately. Her brown cropped hair gracefully framed her face, just as he'd remembered, but what struck him immediately were her eyes. Two superb emerald-green lakes in which he would willingly drown. Without the slightest hesitation, Barbara ran up to Gregory and gave him a friendly hug. He tried hard not to stutter when he said hello.

Mr Griffon shook him firmly by the hand. "Welcome to Brick City! Did you have a good crossing, Gregory?"

"Yes sir, no problem," Gregory replied proudly as he took his place in the rear of the car, beside his pretty friend.

The harbour of Brick City was much like the one at Glassborough. Gregory looked out at the huge yellow cranes that cast their hooks high above the boats moored by the grey quaysides.

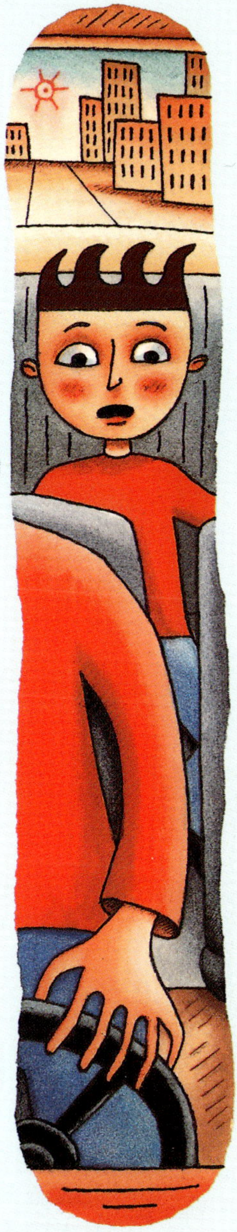

Barbara paid no attention to the view. She had planned lots of things to do with their time. Visits to Brick City's most famous sights, long walks along the coast and, above all, swimming in the sea, from a beach not far from her house. She talked without stopping, and Gregory listened without saying anything. He smiled and shook his head, but it wasn't the view out of the car window that was distracting him now. He was unable to take his eyes off Mr Griffon's hands on the steering wheel. There was no doubt about it, the man had twelve fingers. Each hand had four fingers and a thumb on either side, which gave them a strange fan-like appearance. So? Gregory didn't know why he suddenly felt anxious, but he did.

Absorbed by his thoughts, he suddenly realized that the car had come to a standstill in front of some imposing apartment blocks that towered over the ocean. They had arrived.

The Griffons' home

Barbara immediately took Gregory by the hand and led him to see the room that she had prepared for him. He said nothing, but when they were on the balcony of the room and Barbara stretched out her arm to point out a little island in the far distance, he saw clearly that she too had the same hands as her father – twelve fingers, of which four were thumbs. He felt another sudden stab of anxiety, quickly followed by a feeling of guilt.

"It's just a family thing," he mused, to reassure himself.. "No big deal."

"Greg, I am so happy you were able to come!" Barbara exclaimed as she led him to the kitchen. "We have shared so much in our letters, but to see each other face to face is so much better!"

"Yes, yes, of course!" stammered Greg, who was barely listening to her. He was no longer thinking of the pretty, freckled face, nor of those amazing green eyes. He could think of nothing but those two hands, which disturbed him so much but seemed to cause the Griffons no embarrassment at all.

His unease did not go away. On the contrary.

"So here is the famous Gregory that Barbara is always talking about!" exclaimed Mrs Griffon, holding out her arms in welcome. Gregory couldn't help himself – he could only look at one thing, her hands. Twelve fingers, four of which were thumbs! How could such a phenomenon be possible?

During lunch no one seemed to be aware of Gregory's unease, and he himself, for fear of embarrassing his hosts, took care to avoid gesturing with his hands or saying anything at all about hands, finger or thumbs. Who would have thought it could be so hard?

As soon as they left the table, Barbara decided that they would go for a walk by the sea. In less than an hour, they had reached the little beach which she had often described in her letters. This, she explained to Gregory, was the best place to go for a swim.

On the narrow lane bordered with gorse bushes overlooking the sea, there was only room to walk in single file. Barbara quickened her pace and told her friend many stories on the way down. As Gregory listened, his anxieties began to fade and his hands began to unclench. He looked at Barbara's back and asked himself whether he had really understood before now the important place she had assumed in his life as a result of their correspondence.

Just before they got to the beach, they met a fisherman returning home, with a rod in one hand and a bag slung over his shoulder. As Gregory moved aside to let him pass, he discretely examined the old man's hands. He too had twelve fingers, he too had four thumbs! So it wasn't just a the Griffons...

"Is something the matter?" asked Barbara, as she spread out her bathing towel on the sand. She had just taken off her T-shirt and was facing her friend in her two-piece bathing costume. He seemed to be hypnotized by her stomach.

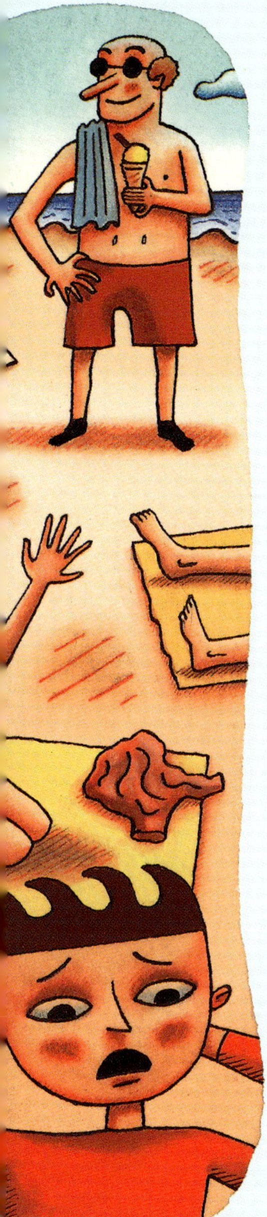

"Aren't you getting undressed?" she asked him, laughing at Gregory's red-faced discomfort.

"Not just now!" he spluttered, looking away and staring hard at the sand. "You go for a swim, and I will catch up with you..."

Barbara was already making her way between the outstretched bodies of the sunbathers. She plunged into the water, giving him a little wave with her hand. That horrible, fan-like hand!

Gregory looked around him. Without exception, every single man, woman and child had twelve fingers, of which four were thumbs! It was absolutely unbelievable! Not only that, but Barbara clearly had two navels as well! Two identical holes, six centimetres apart, in the middle of her stomach! And not just Barbara. All the people spread out on their towels, crossing the beach, returning from their swim or running towards the waves, had not only twelve fingers, but also two navels!

Flee from these monsters!

Gregory panicked. Now he regarded these strangers as aliens. He felt alone and in danger amongst them, lost on his bathing towel like someone shipwrecked and cast up on an island

in the middle of a hostile ocean. Out there in the water, Barbara had stopped swimming and was jumping up and down, calling him to join her. But he no longer saw the lovely girl with whom he had fallen in love from reading her letters. Instead, he saw only the two horrible fans and a stomach pierced with two grotesque holes. How could she have hidden such horrors from him? She, who had recounted to him her life in Brick City down to the last detail. How dared she forget the most important thing of all?

Gregory felt in his pocket and brought out his return ticket for the ferry. Without hesitating, he got up and ran across the beach like a madman, not stopping until he reached the top of the lane and then the main road. The bus driver he hitched a ride with did not ask him any questions. Throughout the ride, Gregory made a supreme effort to avoid letting his glance fall on the driver's hands. He got off at the end of the quays and hurried to where his ferry had docked. At the barrier, the ticket collector changed his ticket, which was dated for the next day, for a card marked 'Immediate Embarkation'. At the quayside, a ferry was getting ready to sail. He only managed to calm himself down when he was on board. He felt like a convict escaping from prison.

Brick City disappeared into the distance. Gregory turned and looked for Glassborough, his home town. When at last he saw it on the horizon, he glanced down at his own hands, resting on the steel rail. Each hand still had four fingers, one thumb.

Gregory felt much better, reassured. He was going home to a town inhabited by normal people with four fingers on each hand, and three navels arranged in a triangle.

Understanding the Human Body

People around the world come in many shapes, sizes and colours, but the human body always follows the same basic design.

In the beginning

Everyone starts as two microscopic cells from their mother and father which join together into one cell. This tiny cell divides thousands of times to produce more than fifty million million cells which make up the human body. Each cell is an individual living unit with a job to do.

Working together

The human body is a complex piece of living machinery made of many different parts. Beneath the skin is a network of muscles and nerves, bones and organs which keeps us alive. It has taken us many centuries to understand how our bodies work. For a long time the processes of digestion, blood circulation and reproduction remained mysteries. Even now we do not understand everything, including all the functions of the brain.

Life story

Each new life begins as a single cell – a tiny fertilized egg which develops into an embryo and then a baby. This baby grows into a child, an adolescent and finally an adult. In much of Europe people can expect to live, on average, to 75 years of age. But in poorer countries a lack of food, clean water and medicines means that life expectancy for some people can be as low as 53 years.

Skin and bark

People in different parts of the world have different ideas about the human body. The Kanakas of New Caledonia believe that trees and people are made of the same thing – the word karo means both 'bark of a tree' and 'the human skin'. The Dogons of Mali believe that the body is a tiny grain of the universe.

An Outer

Your skin is more than just an outer covering – it is the body's largest organ. Its job is to protect your body against infections and injury, and to help keep your body at the right temperature.

Colour control

Everybody's skin contains *melanin,* a pigment (dye) which gives it colour. Differences in skin colour depend on the amount of melanin in the skin – the more melanin, the darker the skin. Melanin protects the skin from damage by too much sun, so people who come from very hot countries usually have dark skin.

Melanin is found not only in your skin but in your hair too. It is also responsible for the colour of the irises in your eyes.

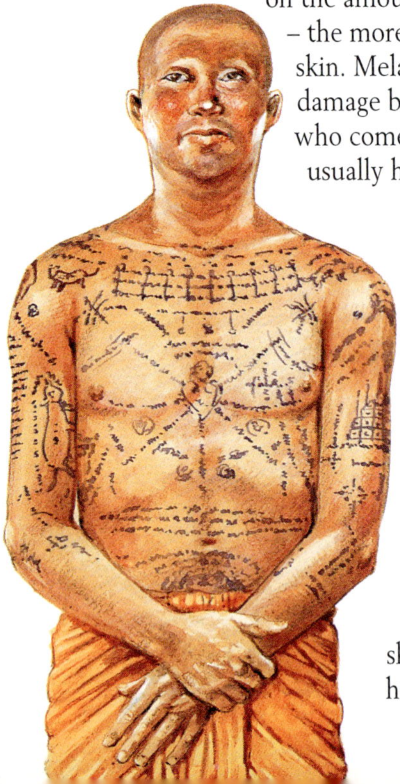

Secret code

The skin on your fingertips is patterned with tiny grooves which give you unique fingerprints. There are nearly six billion (six thousand million) people in the world – every single one of them has a different set of fingerprints. The police use fingerprints to identify people and to find out who was at the scene of a crime.

Painting a picture

Some people have pictures tattooed on their skin. The tattoos are made by puncturing minute holes in the skin and filling them with dyes.

Covering

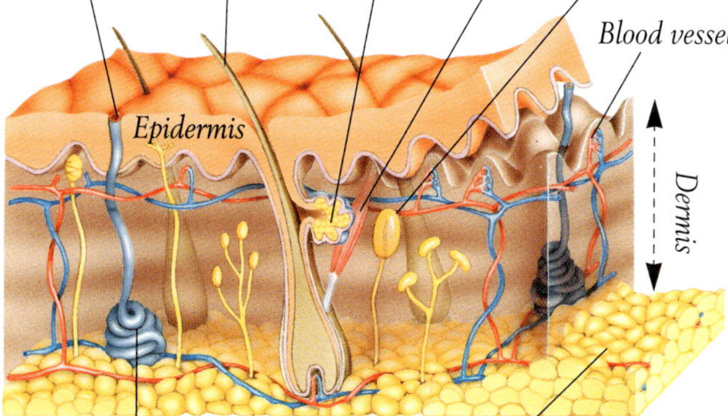

Under the skin

There are two layers of skin. The upper layer, the one you can see, is called the epidermis. It is made up of billions of dead skin cells which eventually flake off, but it is tough and waterproof and protects your body from germs. New cells are made at the base of the epidermis, and these push up to replace the dead cells. The dermis is the lower layer of skin. It contains sebaceous *glands*, which make an oil to soften the skin, and nerve endings, which allow you to detect touch, heat and cold, and pain.

Staying cool

When you get hot, your skin works to cool you down. The pores ooze sweat which then evaporates (dries) and draws heat from your body. Also, the skin's tiny blood vessels widen, allowing more blood to flow through them and lose heat to the air. This is what makes your skin redden.

Glands are found throughout the body. Their job is to produce certain substances that the body needs.

The Skeleton

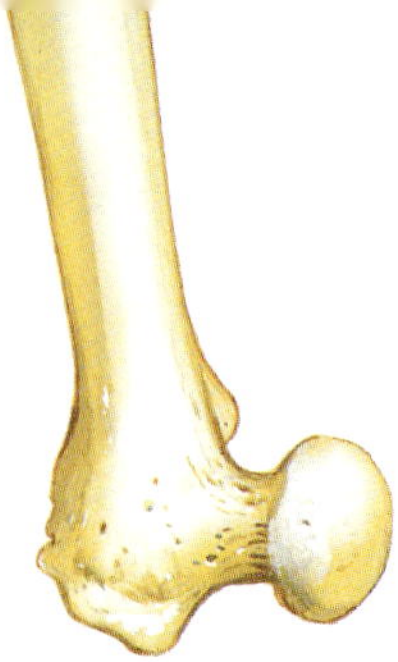

Under your skin, your skeleton has over 200 bones which support your body and protect its organs.

Strong and light

Without a skeleton, you would collapse like a blob of jelly. In order to support your body weight, your bones must be strong. Their strength comes from mineral salts such as calcium, which is found in foods such as milk. Many bones are hollow, which makes the skeleton lighter and easier to move. Many of your bones are linked together at moveable joints such as elbows and knees.

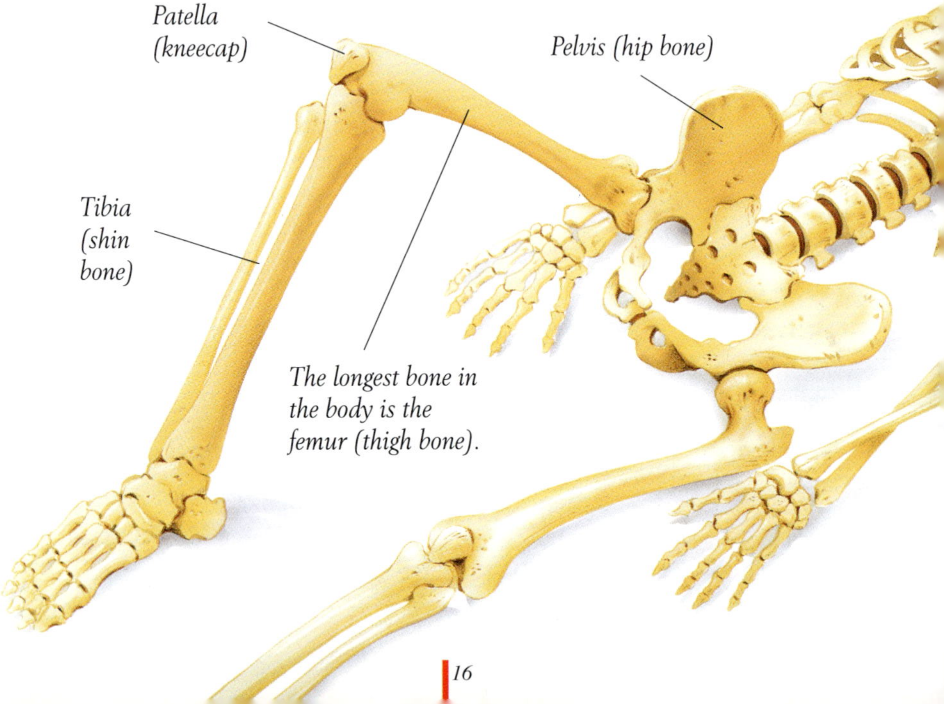

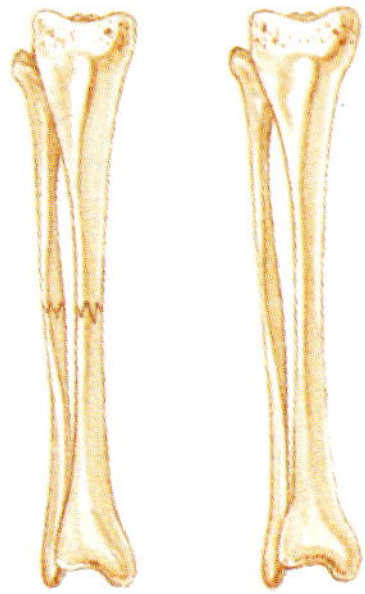

Growing and strengthening

Your skeleton began to develop even before you were born and will continue to develop as long as your body is growing. If a bone is broken, cells inside produce new bone tissue to repair the break. A plaster cast placed round the fracture holds the bone firmly in place while it mends.

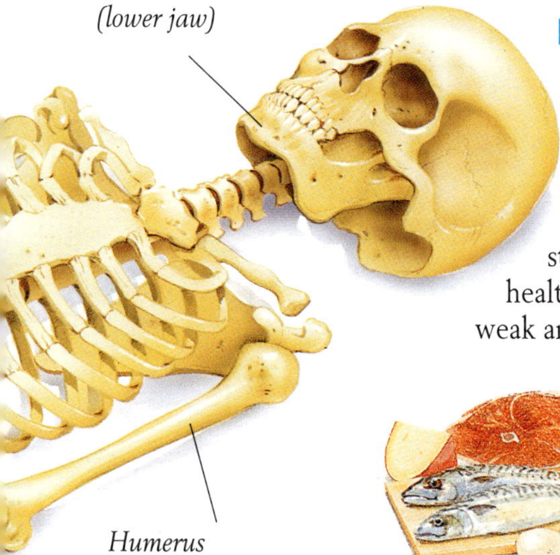

Too weak to work

Some parts of your skeleton protect your vital organs. The skull protects your brain, and the rib cage protects your heart and lungs. *Vitamin D* keeps bones strong and is an important part of a healthy diet. Without it, bones become weak and are more likely to break.

Vitamin D is found in dairy foods, eggs and fish. Skin makes its own vitamin D when it is exposed to sunlight.

Fossils are the remains of once-living material that have been preserved in rock.

The secrets of the past

By studying *fossil* bones, scientists can discover a lot about prehistoric people, including how they walked, what they ate and the diseases they suffered from.

How Do You

The bones in your body are attached to muscles. These muscles move your bones so that you can swim, run, write and talk.

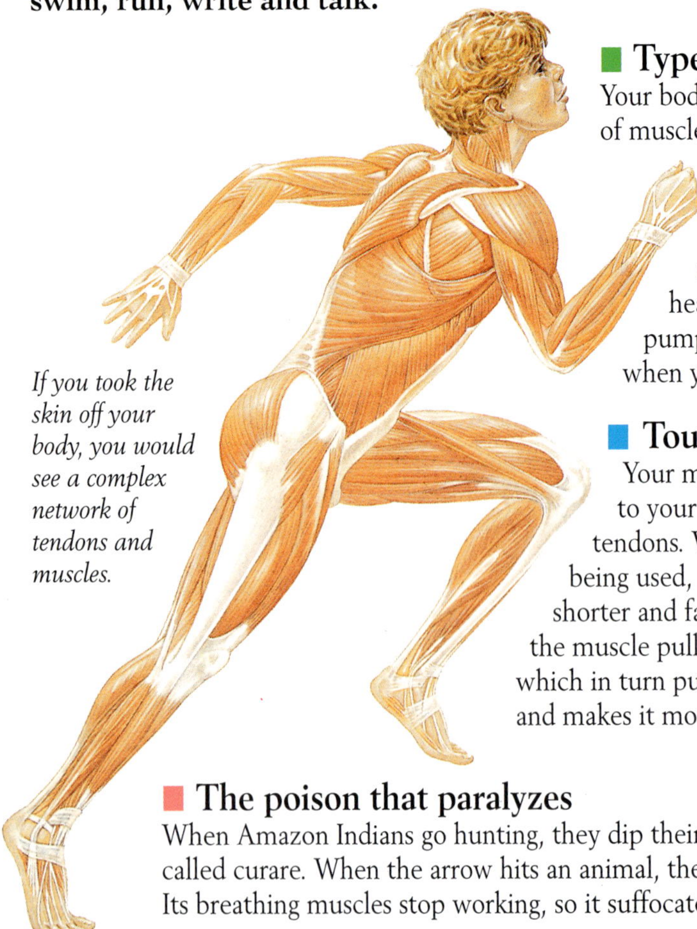

If you took the skin off your body, you would see a complex network of tendons and muscles.

Types of muscle

Your body has two main kinds of muscle. Voluntary muscles work when your brain tells them to. Involuntary muscles, such as the heart muscle that pumps blood, work even when you are asleep.

Tough tendons

Your muscles are attached to your bones by tough tendons. When a muscle is being used, it contracts (gets shorter and fatter). This makes the muscle pull on its tendon, which in turn pulls on the bone and makes it move.

The poison that paralyzes

When Amazon Indians go hunting, they dip their arrows in a poison called curare. When the arrow hits an animal, the poison paralyzes it. Its breathing muscles stop working, so it suffocates and dies.

Move?

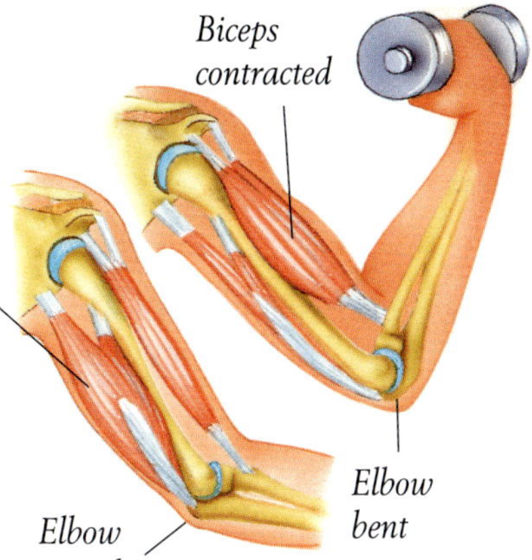

Working together

Muscles work in pairs – when one muscle contracts, the other relaxes. The biceps and triceps muscles are in the upper arm. When the biceps contracts, it pulls up the forearm. When the triceps contracts, the biceps relaxes and the elbow straightens.

When muscles work too hard

When a muscle works too hard, it produces a substance called lactate. This may cause cramp. The cramp can be eased by resting the muscle, stretching it or massaging it. A stitch may be due to cramp of the breathing muscles.

Body-building

Your muscles must be exercised regularly if they are to stay firm and strong and working properly. They soon become weak and waste away if they are not used. Sport helps to build up your muscles – tennis players develop strong arm muscles, and sprinters have very strong leg muscles.

The Nervous

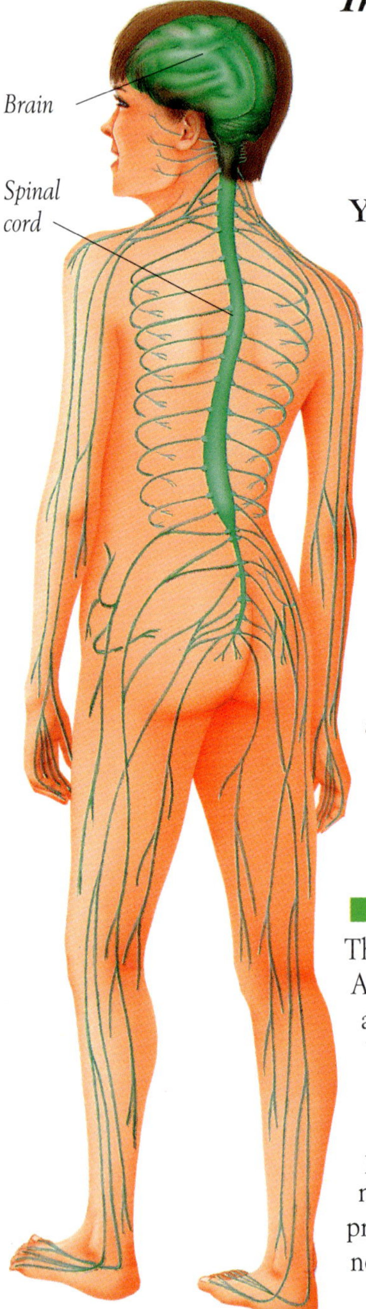

Your body's nervous system is made up of the brain, spinal cord and nerves. It is the brain's job to receive information from, and send back messages to, all parts of the body.

A network of nerves

The nervous system is a huge network of wire-like nerves that reach all parts of the body. The network is linked to the spinal cord that runs through the backbone. This is the main pathway between the nerve network and the brain. Messages are sent along nerves at speeds of up to 100 m per second. That means it is possible for a message to travel the length of your body in a fraction of a second.

Like a computer

The brain is like a very sophisticated computer. A message inputted by the body's senses travels along the nerves as tiny electrical impulses. When this sensory information reaches the brain, the brain processes it and outputs instructions back along the nerves to different parts of the body. These motor signals tell muscles to contract and glands to release their products. Without the nervous system, we could not move, see, speak or do what we do every day.

System

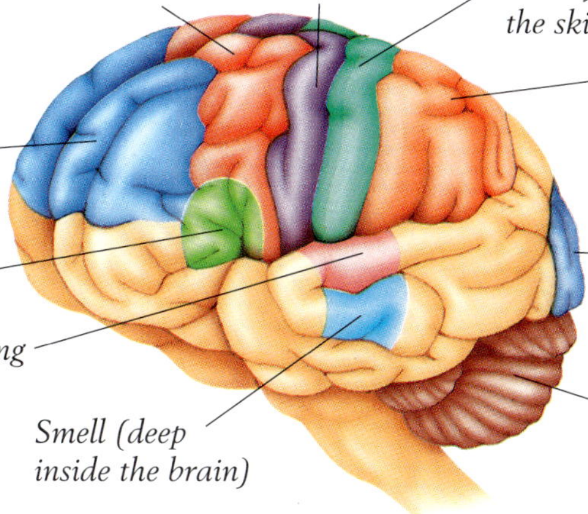

A colour-coded map of the brain

Inside the brain

The brain is a soft, grey organ protected by the skull and is divided into parts which tackle different jobs. For example, messages from the ear are sent to the part that deals with hearing. The right side of your brain controls the left side of your body and vice versa. The brain uses up one fifth of the body's energy even though it only makes up one fiftieth of the body's weight.

Blinking, hiccups and sneezes are reflexes.

Reflex action

If you accidentally touch something hot, you quickly pull back your hand. This is an automatic response called a *reflex*. Temperature receptors in the skin send a message along the nerves to the spinal cord, and an instruction is sent straight back to the muscle in your arm, telling it to contract.

Test Your

Make a reflexometer

You will need:

- a piece of cardboard
- seven felt-tip pens of different colours
- a ruler

1. Cut a strip of cardboard 5 x 35 cm. Rule it off into seven equal parts. Colour each part with a different pen.

How do you use the reflexometer?
Hold it at one end. Tell your friend to have their fingers ready underneath. Let go without warning. The closer to the bottom the reflexometer is caught, the sharper your friend's reflexes!

2. Write something on each part – changing from the most flattering at the bottom to the rudest at the top!

Reflexes

Right or left?

1. Cross your arms. Put the palms of your hands together and cross your fingers.

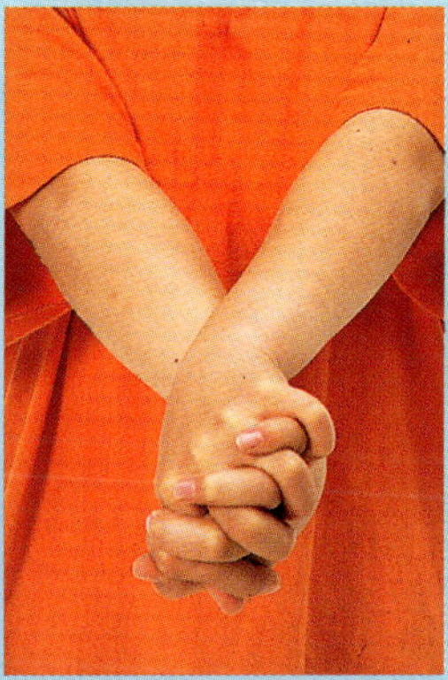

2. Lift your hands towards your chest.

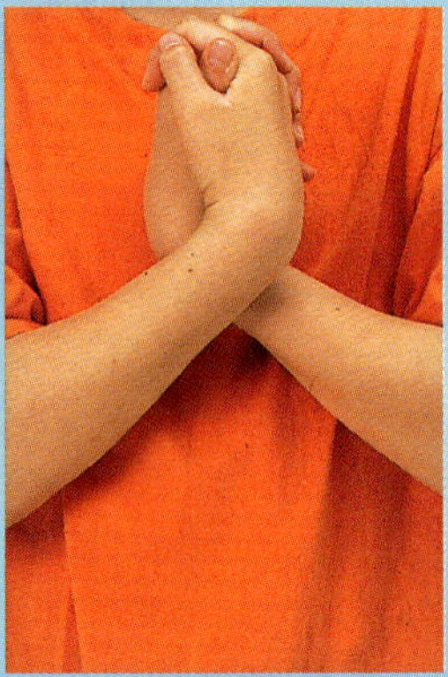

3. Ask someone to tell you — without touching it – which finger you should raise. Do it right away.

It's difficult, isn't it? Your brain sees your left hand where your right hand should be, and vice versa. It is not receiving reliable information from your eyes.

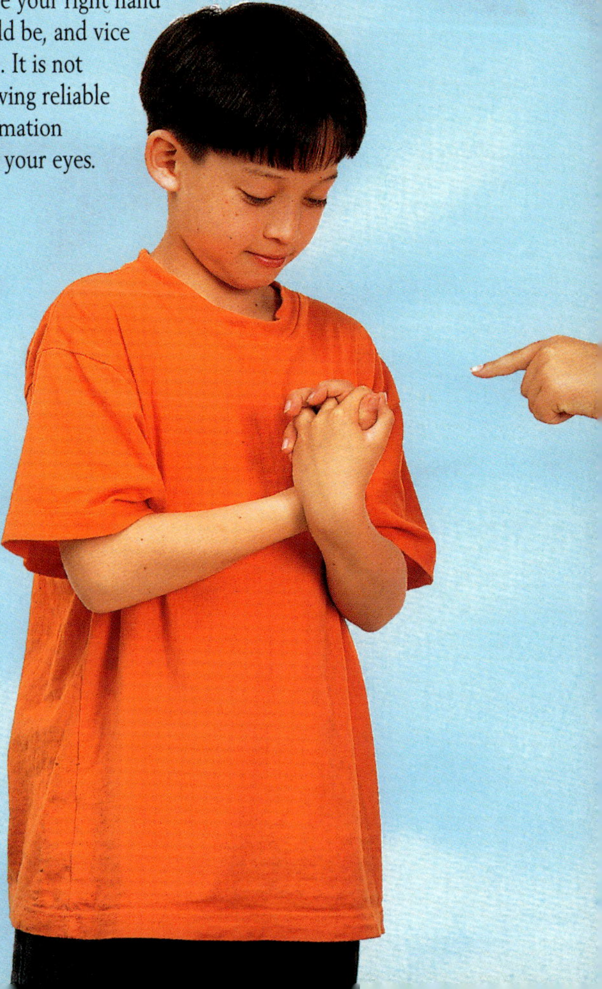

A Healthy

Carbohydrates (starches and sugars)

Proteins

Fats

Food gives you energy and helps you to grow. That is why it is important to eat a healthy diet with plenty of carbohydrates, proteins, fats, fibre, minerals and vitamins.

What's inside?

You get carbohydrates from starchy foods such as rice and sweet foods such as jam. They give you energy. You get proteins from foods such as meat, fish and eggs. They are needed by all parts of your body. Fats give you energy and also make up parts of your cells. The best source are plant foods, such as vegetable oils, and dairy produce, such as butter.

Green vegetables, carrots and tomatoes are rich in vitamin A.

Vitamins and minerals

Fibre, minerals and vitamins

You get fibre mainly from plant foods – it helps you digest your food. You get minerals such as calcium and iron in lots of different foods – they help with the chemical processes in your body. There are six groups of vitamins – A, B, C, D, E and K. Each one has a job to do – for example, vitamin A fights disease and vitamin C is needed for good sight.

Diet

Too little or too much

If you do not eat enough food, or if you fail to get a balanced diet, you can become very ill. In some countries a shortage of food and water means that people may suffer from malnutrition. About 65 percent of your body is made of water – if you had no food and no water, you would die of the lack of water first. You can also become ill if you eat too much food or too much of the wrong food. *Heart attacks* and obesity can both be caused by eating too much of certain fats.

Too much fat, especially fatty animal produce, may cause blood vessels to narrow – in the heart, this can lead to a heart attack.

A balanced meal

Plenty of fibre, vitamins and minerals, and a good mix of fruit and veg

An unbalanced meal

Too many animal fats and sugary foods

You are what you eat

Some foods can change your personality and your behaviour. Coffee contains a lot of caffeine which is a stimulant and can make people hyperactive and irritable.

What Happens to the

When you swallow food, you send each mouthful on an amazing journey through your body. It takes only minutes to eat a meal, but it takes about 24 hours for it to complete its journey through the digestive system.

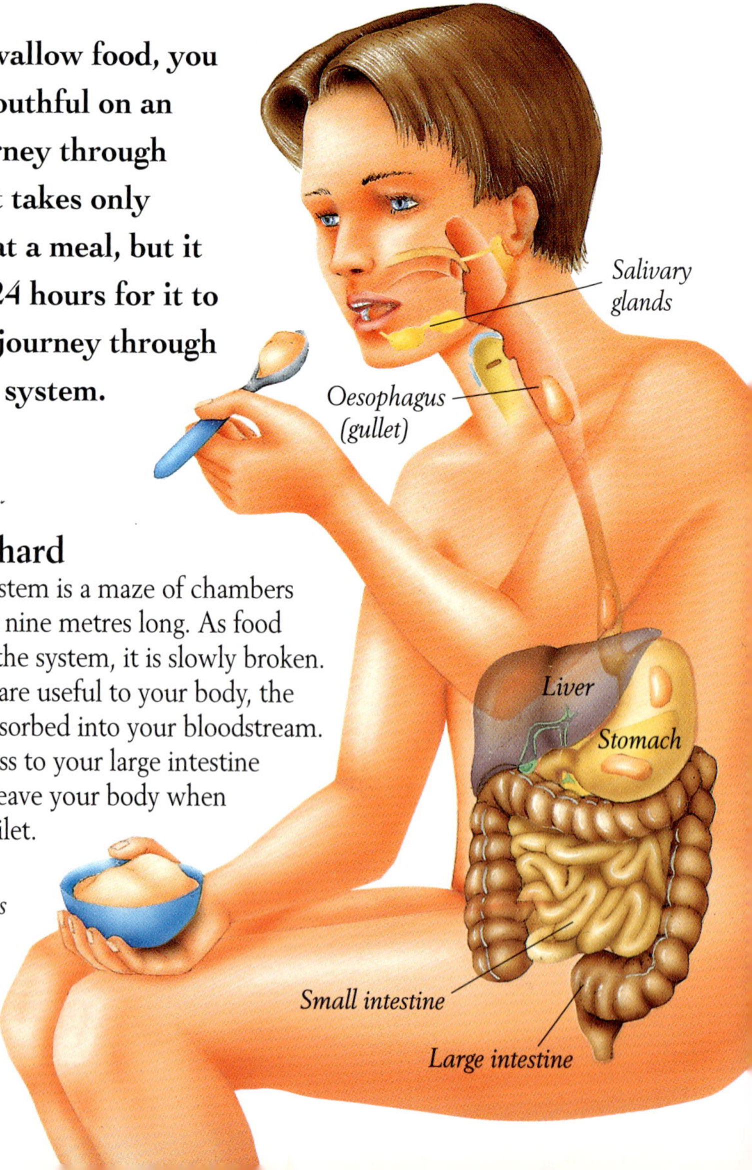

Working hard

The digestive system is a maze of chambers and tubes about nine metres long. As food travels through the system, it is slowly broken. The pieces that are useful to your body, the nutrients, are absorbed into your bloodstream. The leftovers pass to your large intestine and eventually leave your body when you go to the toilet.

Your liver produces a juice called bile. This has enzymes which enter the small intestine to break down the fats you eat.

Food You Eat?

Rude noises!

Gases are released as part of the digestive process, and bubble through your digestive tract – either up and out of the mouth as a burp, or down and out through the anus as you-know-what.

Chomping and chewing

Adults have 32 teeth – 8 incisors, 4 canines, 8 premolars and 12 molars. The incisors (your front teeth) and the canines next to them cut the food, while the premolars and molars at the back grind the food into smaller pieces. Your tongue moves the food around for chewing and swallowing.

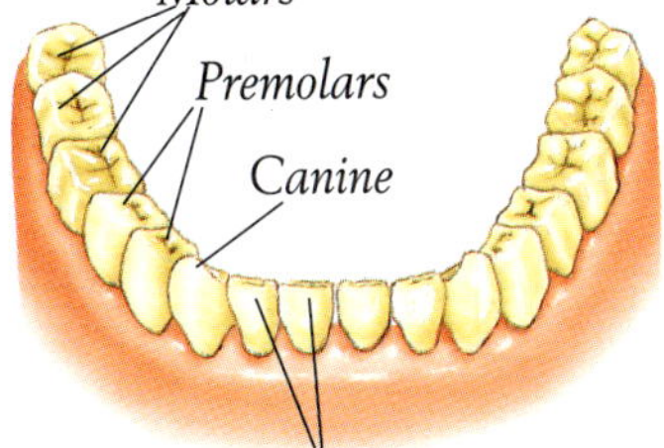

A long journey

It is lunch-time and you are eating a slice of bread. As the bread is chewed, it is mixed with saliva. Saliva contains *enzymes* that break down and dissolve the bread. Muscles in the oesophagus then push the bread downwards. One minute later the bread enters your stomach and is mixed with digestive juices. By being churned like washing in a washing machine, the bread is reduced to a thick soup. Three hours later it is pushed into the small intestine, where it is further digested. Over the next few hours, the bread passes along six metres of small intestine. There it is broken down into sugars, which enter the bloodstream. At about midnight, the remains of the bread pass into the large intestine. Water is removed and the semi-solid waste, called faeces, leaves your body through the anus sometime the next day.

Enzymes are proteins produced by the body. They help break down food by chemical reaction.

How Doe

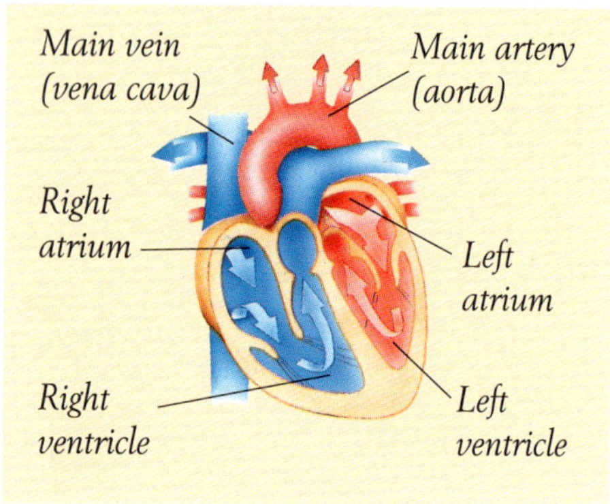

Your heart works 24 hours a day, pumping blood around your body along a network of blood vessels.

On the move

Your heart is about the size of your clenched fist and is made of cardiac muscle. This muscle contracts about 70 times a minute. As it contracts, it pumps blood round the body along a series of blood vessels called arteries, veins and capillaries. Valves work like trap doors to make sure the blood always moves in the right direction. The sound you hear when you listen to someone's heart beating is the sound of the valves slamming shut to stop the blood flowing backwards.

Exercise can increase the heart rate from 70 to 120 beats a minute.

The circulation

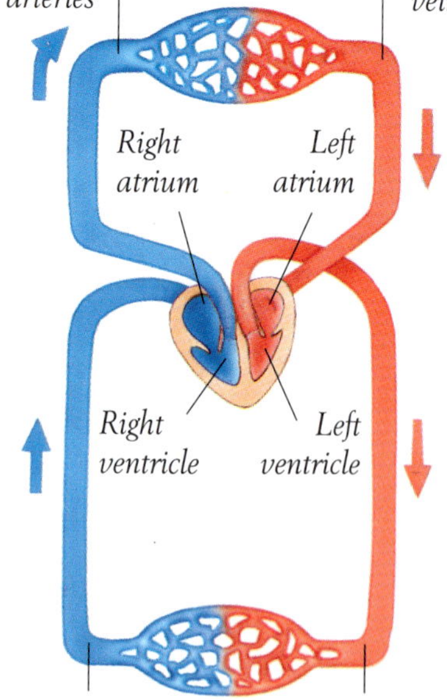

The average adult has 4 to 5 litres of blood, flowing through 100,000 km of blood vessels.

Blood Circulate?

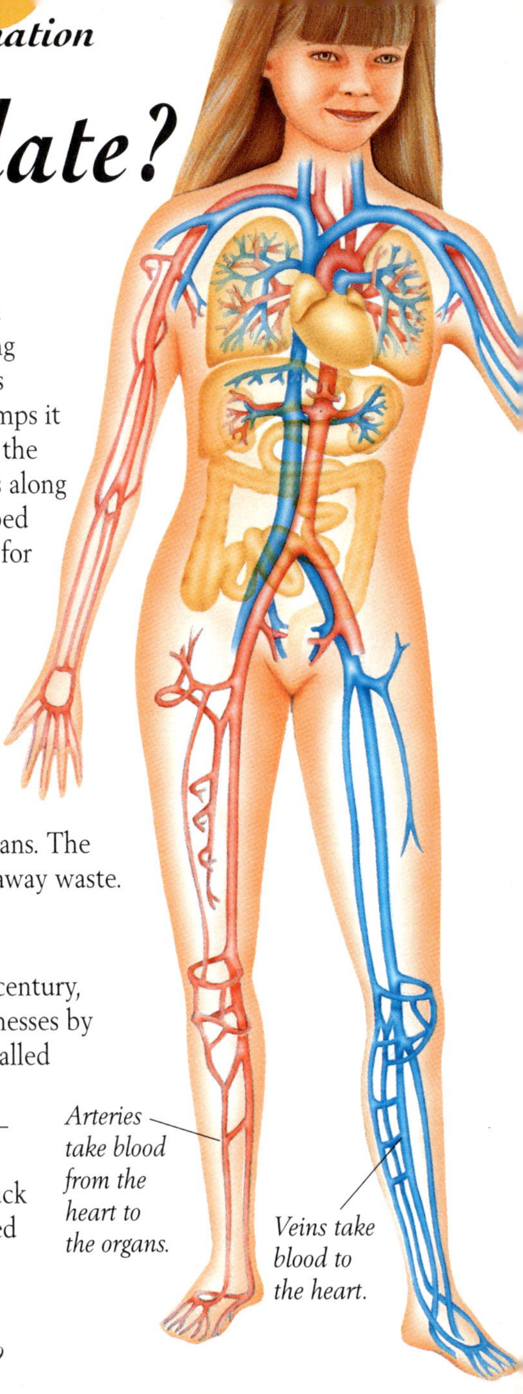

Two sides, two circulations

The heart is in two halves. Each half has a receiving chamber (atrium) and a pumping chamber (ventricle). The left side receives oxygen-rich blood from the lungs and pumps it along arteries to all the body parts except the lungs. The low-oxygen blood then returns along the veins to the heart's right side, is pumped along the pulmonary arteries to the lungs for more oxygen and starts its journey again.

Microscopic vessels

The arteries and veins are connected by thousands of microscopic blood vessels called capillaries. Their walls are so thin that the oxygen in the blood can seep through into the tissues of the body's organs. The blood also supplies nutrients and carries away waste.

A bloody business

From ancient times right up to the 19th century, doctors thought they could heal some illnesses by draining blood from the body. This was called bloodletting. The doctors cut a vein or artery and collected the blood in a basin – sometimes they even placed worm-like creatures called leeches on the skin, to suck out the blood. This ordeal often weakened rather than cured the poor patient!

A Very Peculiar Hospital

Can you spot the twins amongst this turmoil? To help you, here are some clues. One has their long hair tied back. They wear the same tie. One is ill, the other is not.

Solution on p.63

AZI
BEO

Humans, like all animals, need oxygen to live. Each time you breathe in, you take in oxygen from the air. This, together with the food you eat, gives you energy.

Why Do

In and out

Air enters your body through your mouth or nose and flows down your windpipe (trachea) into the lungs. As blood flows through the lungs, it picks up oxygen from the air and releases carbon dioxide. The carbon dioxide is then breathed out.

The diaphragm is a muscle below your lungs. When you breathe in, it contracts and moves down, and air is sucked into your lungs. When you breathe out, your diaphragm expands and moves up, pushing air back out.

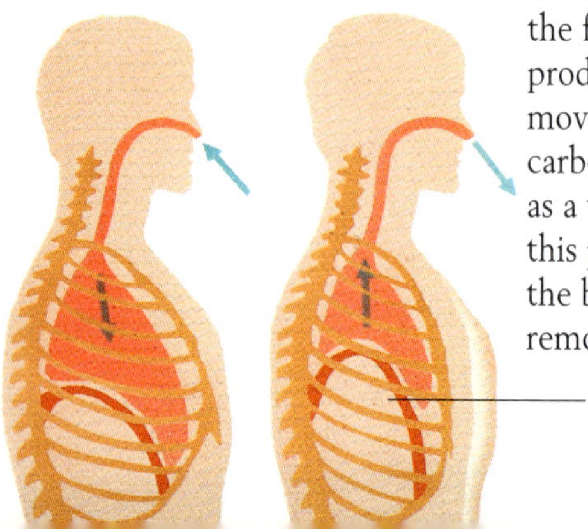

Energy for life

The oxygen you breathe in is carried to every cell of the body. In a process called respiration, the cells use the oxygen to break down sugar in the food you eat, to produce energy to move and live. The carbon dioxide made as a waste product in this process passes into the blood and is removed in the lungs.

You Breathe?

Polluted air

The air in many towns and cities has become polluted by fumes from cars and other vehicles, and this is linked to an increase in asthma cases. Asthmatics have breathing problems because the tubes in their lungs become narrowed, making it difficult for air to flow through them.

Gills instead of lungs

Like all other animals, fish need oxygen. But they get their oxygen from water rather than air, breathing through gills rather than lungs. When they open their mouth and take a gulp of water, the water is forced over the gills. Blood vessels in the gills absorb the oxygen before the water flows out through the gill slits.

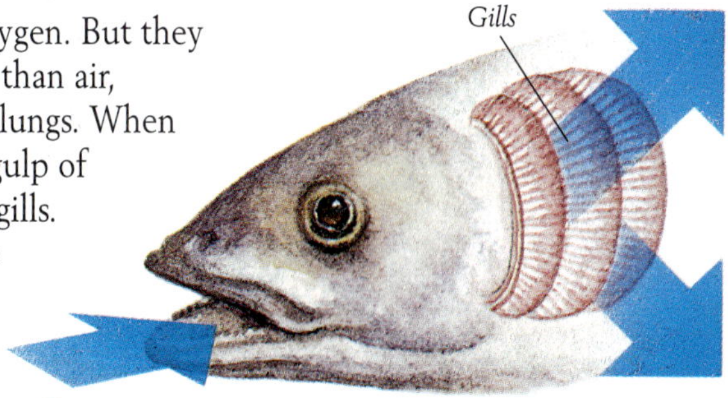

What Do Your Kidneys Do?

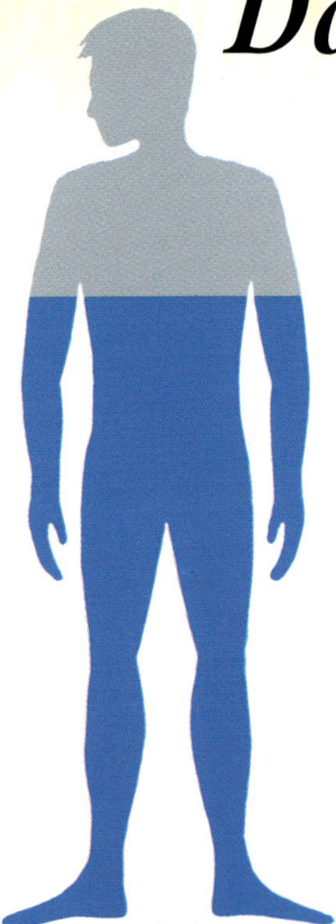

Your body is 65 percent water

You have two kidneys, and their job is to clean your blood and dispose of waste.

Bean-like

Each kidney is about the size of a fist and shaped like a bean. They lie on either side of your backbone, just above your waist.

Filtering the blood

The kidneys clean your blood. Blood flows from the heart into each kidney along an artery. The kidneys filter out the waste products and excess water to make urine. While the filtered blood flows out of the kidneys through veins, the urine is passed to your bladder along a tube called the ureter. When you go to the toilet, the bladder empties the urine down a tube called the urethra.

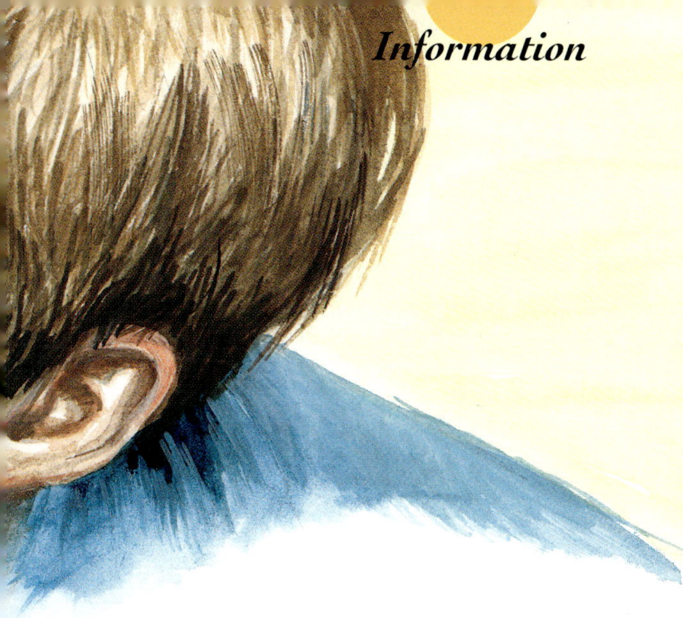

The importance of water

Sixty-five percent of your body is made of water – your kidneys help to keep it at a constant level. It is important to drink enough water every day to help the kidneys wash away waste. People's urine can be studied by doctors to reveal certain illnesses. For example, sugar in the urine could indicate diabetes.

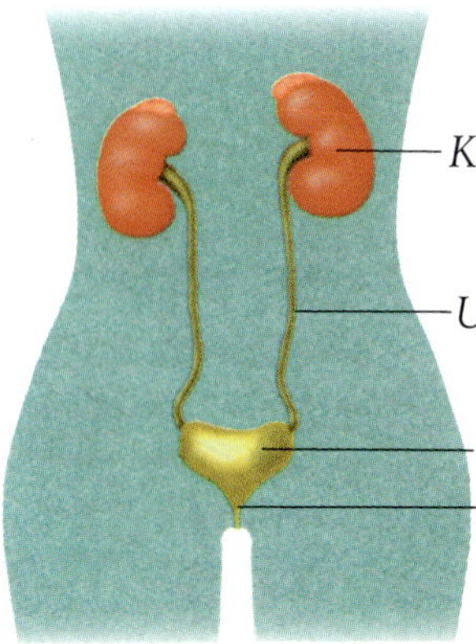

Artificial kidneys

People can lead normal lives with just one kidney, but a patient with two kidneys that don't work properly needs to use a machine to cleanse the blood. This is called a kidney dialysis machine and is usually used three times a week. Patients who need long-term treatment may have a kidney transplant from a donor.

Body

The body is an amazing piece of machinery. It monitors how it is functioning, and adjusts its own internal processes to keep itself alive and healthy.

The story of hormones

Hormones are chemical substances produced by certain glands and carried round your body by the blood. Hormones control the body's chemical processes. The pituitary gland produces over a dozen hormones, one of which controls how big you grow. The adrenal glands produce adrenaline to help you react to dangerous situations.

Controlling glucose levels

Glucose is a type of sugar which is carried round the body in the bloodstream and provides you with energy. There is about one gram of glucose in every litre of blood. If this amount increases or decreases by any significant amount, it can make you very ill. The pancreas keeps your glucose level constant by secreting hormones including insulin. This lowers the level of glucose in the blood. People who are diabetic do not produce enough insulin, so they need injections of insulin to keep their glucose levels healthy.

Controls

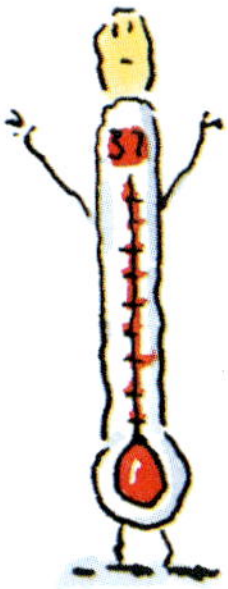

Hot or cold?

Whatever the temperature is outside, your body temperature remains at about 37°C, unless you are unwell. The brain controls your body temperature, in several ways. When you are cold, it makes your muscles twitch, or shiver – this releases heat which the blood spreads through your body. At the same time, the tiny blood vessels in your skin become narrower – this allows less blood to flow through them, and so conserves heat in the body's interior. It also makes your skin look pale. For what happens when you are hot, see page 15.

What about other animals?

Like humans, other mammals and birds too have a constant body temperature. But the temperature of some animals depends on the temperature of their surroundings. Reptiles such as snakes are active only on warm days when they can lie in the sun and absorb heat.

Incredible

SLEEPING UPRIGHT

There is a very odd sleep disorder with the strange-sounding name of narcolepsy. People suffering from the disorder suddenly fall asleep, no matter where they are. Sometimes they fall over because they cannot move their muscles. Fortunately this paralysis is only temporary. Even so, narcoleptics have to be treated with drugs in order to lead a normal life.

MYSTERIOUS MUMMIES

The ancient Egyptians believed that the bodies of the dead needed to be purified for their journey into the afterlife. So they embalmed, or mummified, the bodies. First the embalmers used hooks to churn the brain into a mushy soup that could run out through the nostrils. The space inside the skull was filled with a resin. The organs of the chest and abdomen were removed, and the body was covered in salt for 40 days to dry out its fluids. Then the cavities were stuffed with cloths. Finally, the body was wrapped in bandages and given a life-like mask. It was placed in a series of coffins, and sealed in a tomb for ever.

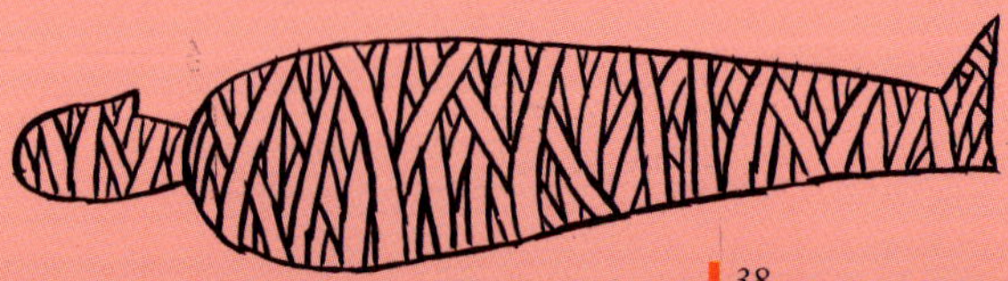

but True!

RECORDS FOR LONG LIFE

In the 1950s, at Vilcambra, a small village in South America, a number of centenarian Indians were discovered. Some of them had reached an amazing 120 years of age. Researchers discovered that conditions in the village – the high altitude, the climate, the vegetarian diet – all contributed to a long and healthy life. Since then, many have visited the village in in search of the secret to a long life. Although a Brazilian woman claims to 126 year old, the official record for the longest life is held by a French woman who was 122 years old when she died. The oldest man is 115-year-old American.

AN AMAZING MONK

Abbot Lazzaro Spallanzani lived in Italy around 1780. He conducted some curious experiments to unravel many of the mysteries of digestion. For example, he took some liquid from the stomach of a bird and put it into small metal tubes containing either meat or seed. To keep the mixtures at body temperature, he placed the tubes in his armpits for three days! In another experiment, he swallowed small tubes containing different foods. There were holes in the tubes to allow his digestive juices to get at the food. He then recovered the tubes when they left his body with his faeces. The results of the abbot's studies contributed greatly to our understanding of digestion.

Protecting Your Body

Your body's defence system is always on the alert, ready to protect you against invading germs and other forms of disease.

Medical scientists called bacteriologists study bacterial germs under a microscope to identify different kinds and then develop drugs to kill them.

Bacteria and viruses

Germs are harmful micro-organisms or microbes, so called because they can be seen only through a microscope. Viruses are the smallest of all germs and cause diseases such as influenza and measles. Bacteria are larger germs that cause diseases such as tonsillitis and tetanus. Once a harmful germ gets inside the body, it takes over the body's cells and multiplies, damaging the cells and making you feel ill. This is called an infection.

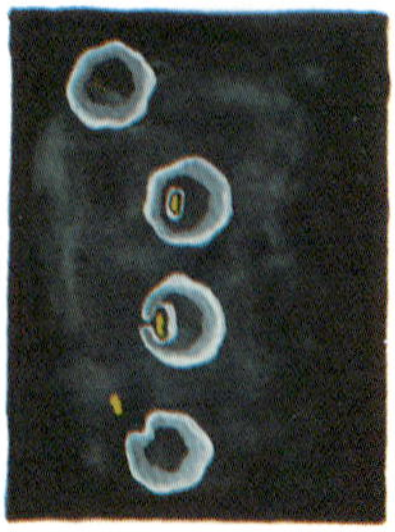

White blood cells engulf bacteria.

Germ invasion

Micro-organisms are everywhere – in water, in the air, on your skin and even inside you. Most are harmless – some are even used to make food such as cheese. But harmful ones can be breathed in, swallowed or taken in through cuts in the skin. One way your body fights back is to send in an army of white blood cells to attack the germs.

Fooling germs

In 1796, English scientist Edward Jenner noticed that people who contracted a disease called cowpox rarely suffered from the similar disease, *smallpox*. He realized that a person could be protected against a disease by being injected with dead or weakened versions of the offending germs. The vaccine tricks the body into thinking that it is under attack, so that it is prepared to fight when the real germs come along.

Smallpox was a highly infectious disease that has been wiped out by vaccination.

Killing bacteria

In 1929, Alexander Fleming discovered that certain moulds could kill bacteria. The active ingredient in the moulds was an antibiotic called penicillin. Since his discovery, more antibiotics have been found which kill bacteria.

Very rarely, some people are born without any defence against germs. They must live in a sterile (germ-free) room until they can be cured.

The Importance

During your life, you will spend more than one third of your time asleep. Sleep is vital for your health, and without it you would die within a few weeks.

The sleep cycles

Scientists have discovered that every night you go through different stages of sleep. Each complete cycle takes about 100 minutes. First you fall into a light sleep. This sleep gradually gets deeper until you fall into a deep sleep, when it becomes difficult to wake you. After a period of deep sleep, you move into a phase of light sleep again. This cycle of deep and light sleep is repeated several times before you wake up. Scientists use a machine called an EEG to show brain waves during sleep to see how active the brain is at different stages.

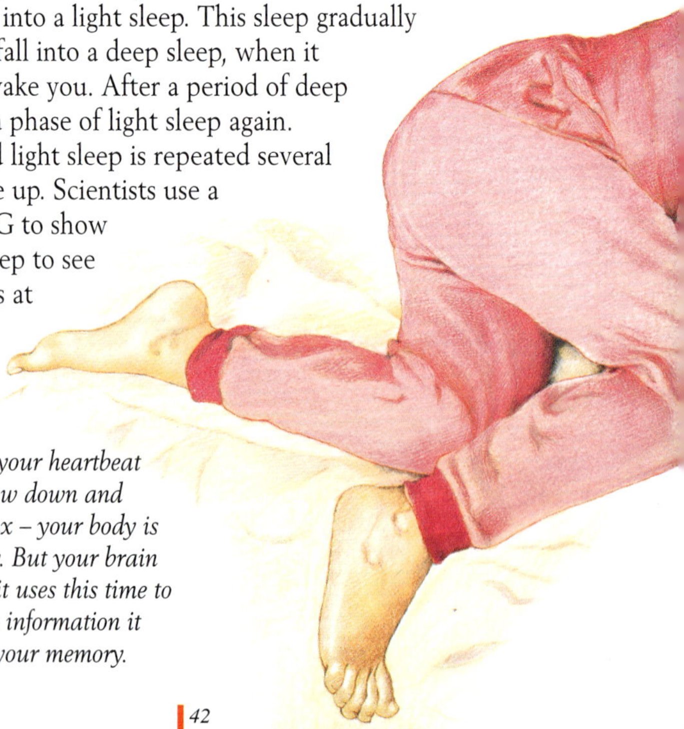

While you sleep, your heartbeat and breathing slow down and your muscles relax – your body is conserving energy. But your brain is still busy, and it uses this time to process any extra information it needs to store in your memory.

# of Sleep

Dream time

During one stage of sleep, your eyes flutter behind your eyelids. This is called REM or rapid eye movement. It is during this stage that you dream. You probably have about five dreams every night – although you may never remember them! You are only likely to remember a dream if you are woken up during REM.

Different animals need different amounts of sleep. A horse sleeps for only two to three hours, while a bat needs up to 20 hours sleep.

Scientists have calculated that by the end of a busy day you may have shrunk by one centimetre. Don't worry, with a good night's sleep you get back to your normal height.

The body temperature of an animal which hibernates (sleeps through winter) drops several degrees.

Time to recharge

Everybody needs sleep. During sleep, our bodies relax and recover from the busy day. Babies spend up to 20 hours a day asleep, but as we get older we need less sleep. An eight-year-old child needs about 10 hours of sleep, while an adult usually needs less than eight hours.

The Five Senses

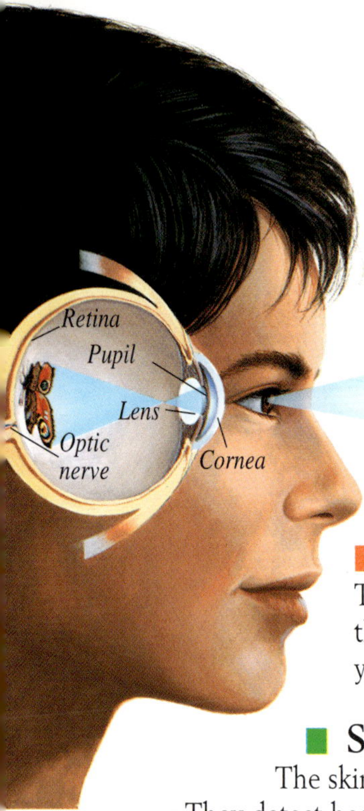

The body's five main senses detect changes in the outside world and send information to the brain. These five senses are touch, sight, taste, smell and hearing.

The sense messengers

The brain receives a constant stream of messages from all the sense organs – your skin, your eyes, your tongue, your nose and your ears.

Skin to touch with

The skin has sensory receptors that give you a sense of touch. They detect heat and cold, pain, pressure and vibrations. The fingertips are especially sensitive and are used by blind people to read Braille.

Eyes to see with

Your eyes give you a view of the outside world. Light reflected from objects passes through the pupil and lens. When it hits the retina at the back of the eye, an upside-down image forms. The optic nerve carries a message to the brain, where the image is turned the right way up.

The human eye sees a white daisy and green grass, but a bee sees blue-green daisies and pale yellow grass!

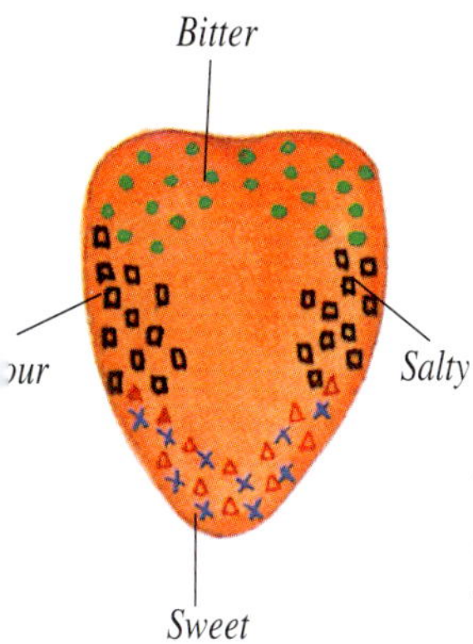

A tongue to taste with

Your tongue is covered in microscopic taste buds which detect the flavour of food. The taste buds can recognize four main tastes – sour, bitter, sweet and salty. Each area of the tongue is sensitive to one of them. From different combinations, you can recognize hundreds of flavours.

A nose to smell with

Your nose can detect thousands of smells from chemicals floating in the air. Smell can also affect taste. If you have a blocked nose from a cold, it is hard to smell or taste food.

Ears to hear with

The ears receive sounds from vibrations, or sound waves, in the air. The outer ear sends sounds to the eardrum, making it vibrate. The vibrations then push on three tiny bones (the hammer, anvil and stirrup), making them move. The sounds continue into the fluid-filled cochlea tube and when the fluid moves, it pushes on the sensory cells, which send messages to the brain.

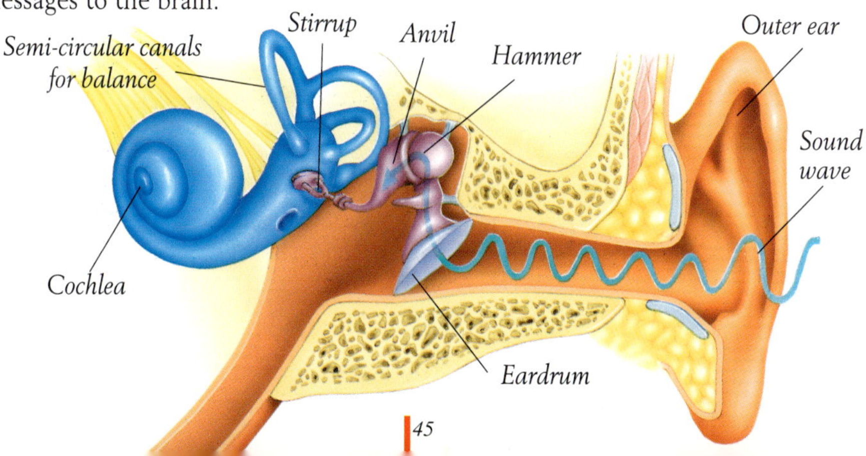

Testing Your

Sight

You will need:
- a coin
- pot

Stand about 70 cm away from a open pot Cover one eye. Ask someone to follow your instructions ("Left a bit, right a bit..") before dropping a coin into the pot. It is surprising how two eyes are so much better than one!

Taste and smell

You will need:
- some cheese, a carrot and an apple
- a knife,
- a scarf

1. Cut the food into small cubes.

2. Cover your partner's eyes with the scarf and tell him to pinch his nose.

3. Let him taste each type of food. Then change places. Can you tell what you are tasting?

Senses

Hearing

Stand about 30 m away from a friend. Ask them to tap on a wall with a stick. Watch and listen carefully. You will see the stick touch the wall, but the sound will follow a short time afterwards.

Touch

1. Cut out some cards and draw letters on each of them.

2. Following the lines of the letters, use a sharp pencil to pierce small holes at regular intervals.

3. Blindfold one of your friends and give them the cards to 'read'. You could also make whole words in the same way.

Making a New Life

Every human being begins as a single cell – a fertilized egg. This cell is created when a tiny egg inside the mother is fertilized by a sperm from the father.

Inside a man

From *puberty* until death, a man produces sperm, the male sex cells, in his two testicles. He produces about 500 million new sperm every day, but only one will be needed to fertilize a woman's egg.

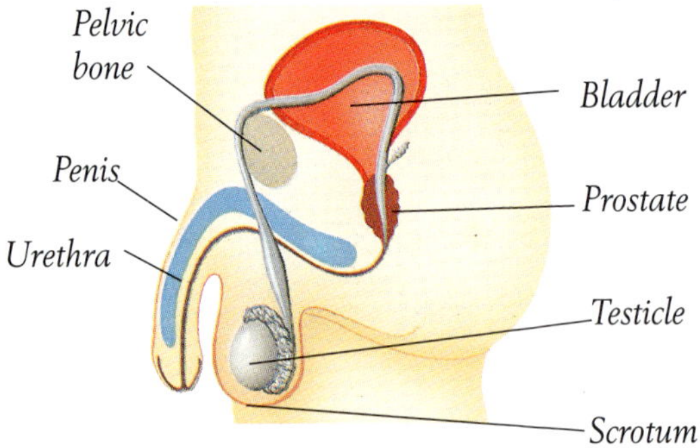

Puberty is the time in life when a child's body changes and develops into that of an adult.

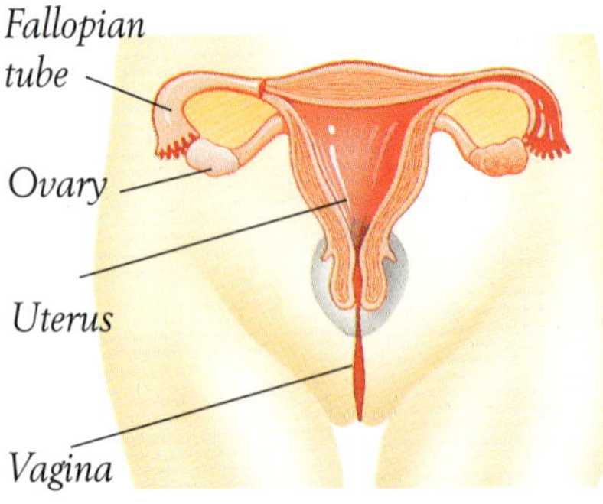

Inside a woman

In her abdomen, a woman has two ovaries that make eggs, the female sex cells. When a girl reaches *puberty*, one of her ovaries releases an egg once a month into her fallopian tubes. The uterus (womb) gets ready to receive the egg by thickening its walls with blood. If it is fertilized, the egg will need nutrients from the blood.

The menopause happens at about 50 years of age, when a woman's ovaries stop releasing eggs. She can no longer conceive a baby.

Monthly periods

If the woman's egg is not fertilized, the lining of the uterus comes away and leaves the body through the vagina. This is called a period, or menstruation. It takes place about every 28 days.

Making love

To make a baby, the man's sperm cells must be placed inside the woman, so that one of them can fertilize her egg cell. During love-making, the man places his penis inside the woman's vagina and ejects a liquid filled with sperm. The sperm swim through the uterus to the egg. Millions of sperm start the journey, but only one will fertilize the egg and start its development into a baby.

Where do babies come from?

People used to believe that babies were a gift from heaven. It was not until the 18th century that scientists realized that an egg and a sperm had to fuse in order to produce a baby.

Inside the

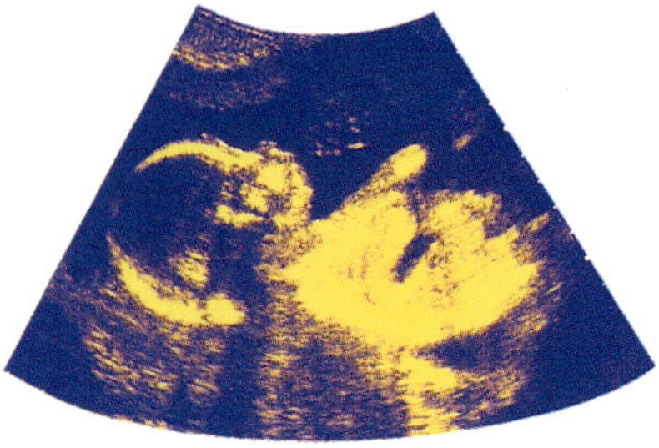

An ultrasound scan

It takes nine months for a fertilized egg to develop into a baby ready to be born.

From cell to embryo to baby

The fertilized egg cell multiplies over and over again to become a ball of cells which begins to take shape as an embryo. During the following months, its features gradually develop and the embryo looks more and more like a baby. After just three weeks, its organs begin to form and its heart starts beating. By the eighth month, the baby prepares itself for birth by positioning itself with its head pointing down. *Ultrasound scans* allow doctors to check the baby is healthy during pregnancy.

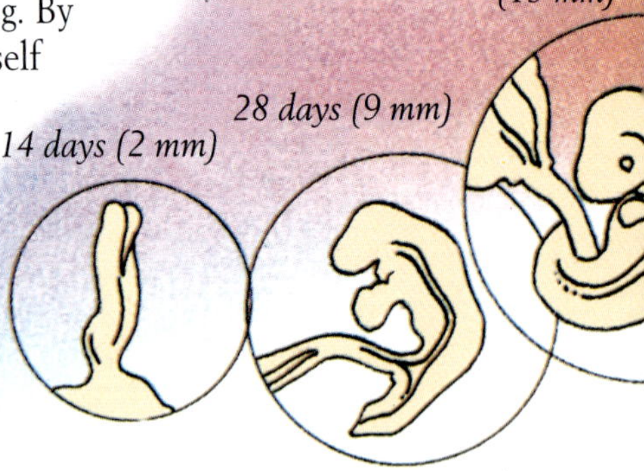

An ultrasound scanner uses sound waves to see the unborn baby in the mother's womb.

Twins

Sometimes two babies are born from the same egg. This creates identical twins who look exactly alike. Non-identical twins come from two eggs that are each fertilized by a different sperm at the same time. They may not look the same and they may be different sexes. About one in 80 births produces twins.

Womb

Feeding the unborn baby

While the baby is in the womb, it receives oxygen and food from the placenta along the umbilical cord. When the baby is born, the cord is cut and what remains is tied in a knot to become your belly button.

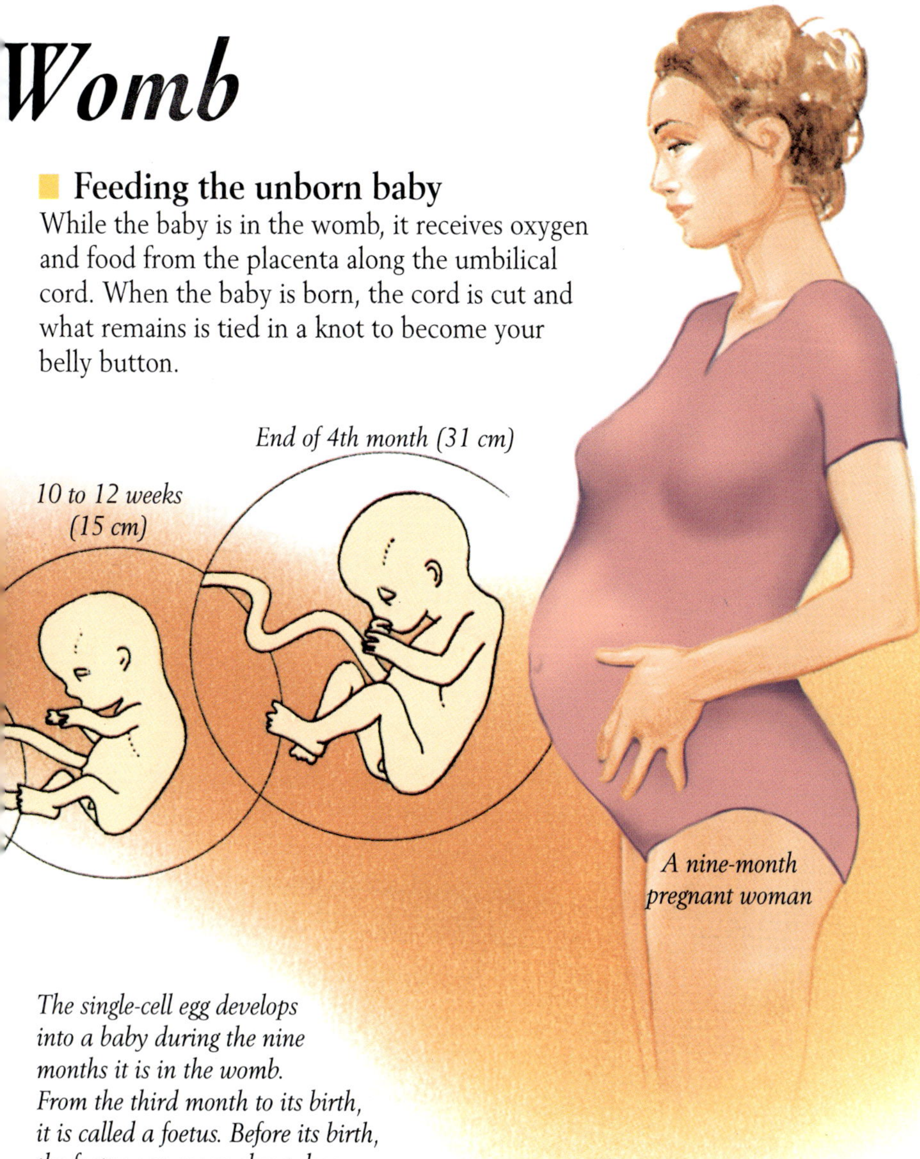

The single-cell egg develops into a baby during the nine months it is in the womb. From the third month to its birth, it is called a foetus. Before its birth, the foetus can move about, hear loud noises and suck its thumb, but it spends most of its time asleep.

The First Minutes of Life

After nine months, the mother's body begins to signal that her baby is ready to be born.

Ready to be born

The mother first knows her baby is ready to be born when she feels the muscles in her womb squeeze. These squeezes are called contractions and can be painful. The contractions grow more frequent and stronger, and in the final stages they help push the baby out of the womb and the vagina (birth canal).

The birth

Giving birth can be very quick or take many hours. The baby's head usually comes out first, followed by its body. The baby gulps its first breath of air, often crying to help open up the airways in its lungs. It is ready for its first feed, usually milk from its mother's breasts, while mother and baby rest and get to know each other by sight, smell, sound and touch.

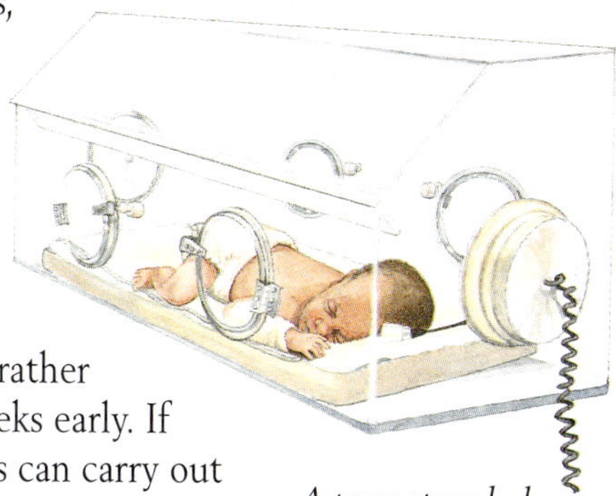

A premature baby in an incubator

Problems at birth

Sometimes the birth does not go as planned. The baby's legs may appear first, rather than its head, or it may be born several weeks early. If there are difficulties with the birth, doctors can carry out a Caesarean operation. The doctor opens the mother's abdomen and removes the baby from the uterus. Babies born too early are placed in an incubator until they grow bigger and stronger. The incubator keeps the baby warm, with plenty of oxygen, nourishment and contstant care.

Looking like your parents

What the baby looks like is largely determined by a set of instructions that were passed on from its mother and father to the fertilized egg. These instructions are called genes and they help decide things such as whether the baby will have dark or light hair, blue eyes or brown. Because these genes have come from the mother and father, the baby will often look like them.

Looking after

Good health depends on looking after yourself sensibly and not doing things that harm your body or damage the way it works.

Keeping fit

One way to stay healthy is to take regular exercise. Exercise keeps your muscles firm and helps your organs, particularly your heart and lungs, to work better. Playing sport, cycling, swimming, dancing – even walking to school – are all good forms of exercise. So start today – getting fit and staying fit will be fun.

Fighting germs

There are always germs living on your skin and generally they do no harm. But if germs get into your body, they can make you ill. Germs can get on to food from dirty hands, so it is important to wash your hands before meals and after going to the toilet. Germs also grow on bits of food left in between your teeth. Get rid of them by brushing your teeth after meals and before you go to bed at night.

Yourself

Avoiding harmful substances

Doctors prescribe drugs as medicine to make sick people better. But some young people use other kinds of drugs that are seriously dangerous to their health. They take the drugs to feel better about themselves, to be less shy, or to feel they belong to a group. In time, they may become so addicted to the drugs that they cannot live without them.

People who smoke cigarettes become breathless and may have a cough. That's because they are taking tar, nicotine and poisonous gases into their body. These can also cause heart disease and lung cancer.

People who drink too much alcohol don't just get noisy and stagger about – they may eventually damage their liver.

You can enjoy life so much more if you stay well – so it really is better to avoid all of these harmful substances.

Not too much sun

It's fun to be on the beach or in the park on a hot summer's day. But don't forget sunlight contains ultraviolet light that can burn the skin and may cause skin cancer. So when you are out in the sun, you should protect your skin with suncream or cover up with some more clothing.

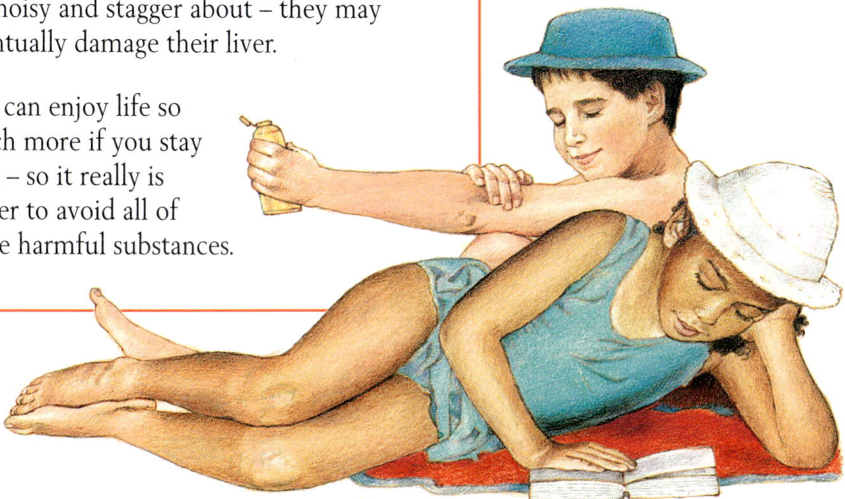

Growing Up

Once a baby is born, it continues to change and develop, as it did in the womb. First the baby develops quickly into a child and then, before adulthood, the child goes through puberty.

Hormones take charge

Puberty takes place at some time between the ages of about 10 and 16 for girls, 12 and 17 for boys. It prepares the body for parenthood by developing the sex organs. The brain produces hormones which travel in the bloodstream all around the body, triggering the changes. These changes occur slowly over a couple of years, during a time known as adolescence.

During adolescence, people go through emotional as well as physical changes – they begin to feel differently about themselves and other people. This is when boys and girls begin to be attracted to each other.

Changes in boys

One of the first signs of puberty in boys is hair growing on the lower half of the face. Hair also grows around the sex organs and under the armpits. The penis becomes larger and the voice 'breaks', becoming much deeper. The body also grows quickly, becoming much taller and more muscular.

Changes in girls

When girls reach puberty, they start to develop breasts and grow hair under their armpits and in the groin. They also grow taller and their hips become wider. The major change they experience is the start of their periods, which occur for a few days each month.

Adolescence

The body's increased production of sex hormones can cause problems for teenagers, such as acne or spots. There may also be personality changes that result in moodiness. Fortunately, these changes are usually temporary and just mark the change to adult life. The body finally stops growing at about 20 years old.

True or

The contractions of the heart are voluntary rather than automatic.

False. You don't have to think about them. Your heart contracts on its own for 24 hours a day.

The liver has nothing to do with digestion.

False. Your liver produces bile, which you need for the digestion of fats.

The red blood cells are made in the marrow of some bones.

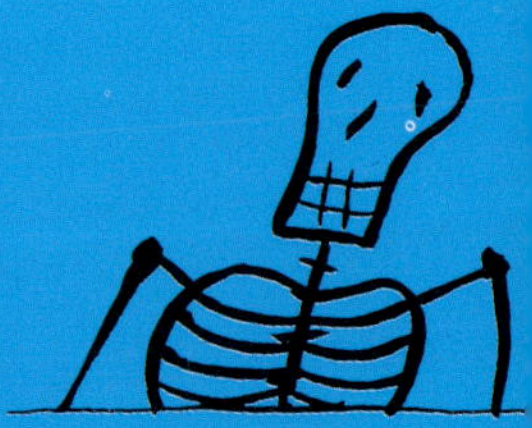

True. Red blood cells are made in the bone marrow of bones such as the skull, vertebrae, ribs and hips.

An adult has fewer bones than a child.

True. As a small child develops, some bones fuse together to form one larger bone, for example the skull.

False?

Colour blind people confuse red and yellow.

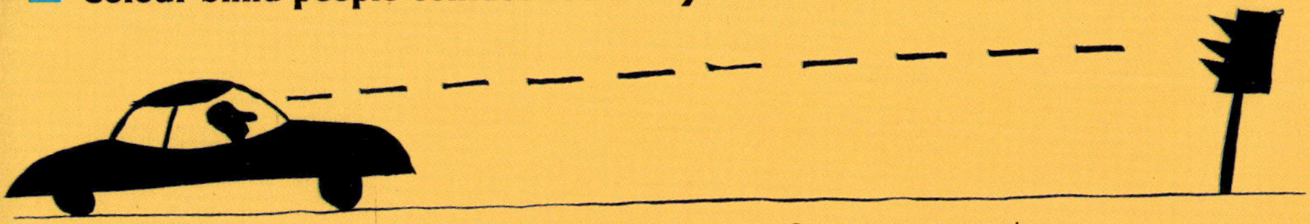

False. A colour-blind person cannot distinguish between red and green.

Short-sighted people cannot see distant objects clearly, whereas long-sighted people have trouble seeing near objects.

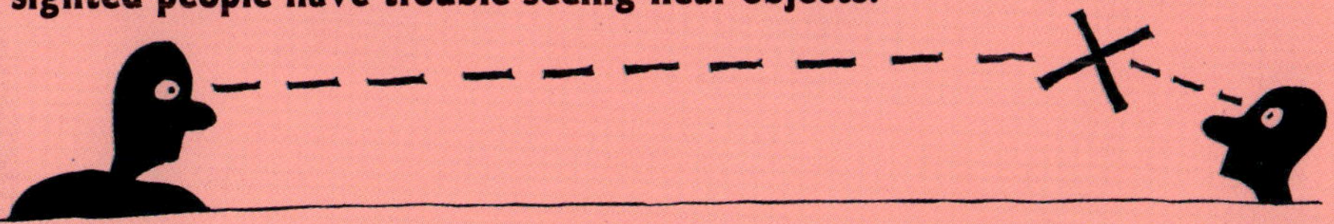

True. Both groups of people can solve the problems by wearing glasses or contact lenses.

Smoking can cause heart disease.

True. The nicotine in cigarettes affects the functioning of the heart.

Antibiotics are medicines that kill viruses.

False. Antibiotics are only effective against bacteria.

A Test

True o

Your blood's sugar level can vary considerably without risk to your health.

False. The sugar level must be kept within a very narrow range. Too low or too high is dangerous.

Oxygen is carried by white blood cells to all the cells of your body.

False. Only the red blood cells carry oxygen.

When you sneeze, the air leaves your nose at about 160 km per hour.

True. Sneezing clears irritating dust and mucus from your nose.

You cannot be vaccinated against the disease tetanus.

False. There is a vaccine against the bacteria causing tetanus, which can enter the body if you cut yourself gardening or doing DIY.

False?

Water is an essential part of your body.

True. Water makes up about 65 percent of your weight. If you weigh 35 kg, you contain 22.7 kg of water.

Good sources of protein are pasta, rice and bread.

False. These foods are rich in starch. Protein is found in meat, fish and eggs.

The navel is the scar from the umbilical cord that links a baby to the placenta in the mother's uterus.

True. This scar stays with you for your whole life.

An adult's body is made up of 50 million cells.

False. There are billions of cells in the human body.

Index

Solution to the game on pages 30-31

Created by Marie-Odile Fordacq
Authors Hubert Ben Kemoun, Brigitte Dutrieux, Catherine Pauwels
Managing Editors Marie-Odile Fordacq, Camilla Hallinan
Editorial co-ordinators Max Benato, Ariane Léandri, Molly Perham
Art editors Sue Aldworth, Ch'en Ling, Bernard Girodroux, Val Pidgeon
Illustrators David Ashby, Shirley Bellwood, Ian Chamberlain, Peter Dennis, Éric Doxat, Jeff Fisher, Chris Forsey, Pamela Goodchild, Daniel Guerrier, Nick Hall, Sophie Jacopin, Christian Jégou, Urs Landis, Olivier Lemoine, Ruth Lindsay, Nathalie Locoste, Denise et Claude Millet, Michael Sheehy, Étienne Souppart, Pat Tourret, Richard Ward, Joanna Williams
Activities Ting Morris, Tim Ridley Photography, Val Wright
Photo research Veneta Bullen
Photo credits Bridgeman Art Library (Museum of Fine Arts, Budapest), James Davis Travel Eye Ubiquitous, Mary Evans, Getty Images, Petit Format, Science Photo Library
Design and page make-up Équipage, Olivier Lemoine, Judy Linard, Terry Woodley
Consultant Steve Parker

KINGFISHER
An imprint of Kingfisher Publications Plc
New Penderel House, 283–288 High Holborn, London WC1V 7HZ

This edition first published by Kingfisher Publications Plc 1998
Originally published in France by Nathan
under the title *Megascope: Le corps humain exploré*

2 4 6 8 10 9 7 5 3 1

A CIP catalogue record for this book is available
from the British Library

ISBN 07534 0 0223 8

Printed in Italy

Stickers

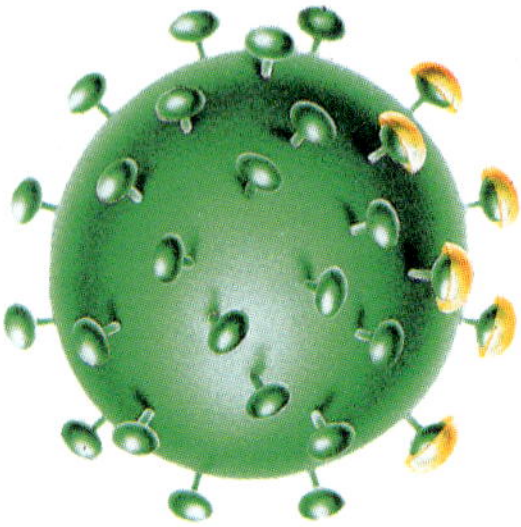

A virus in close-up

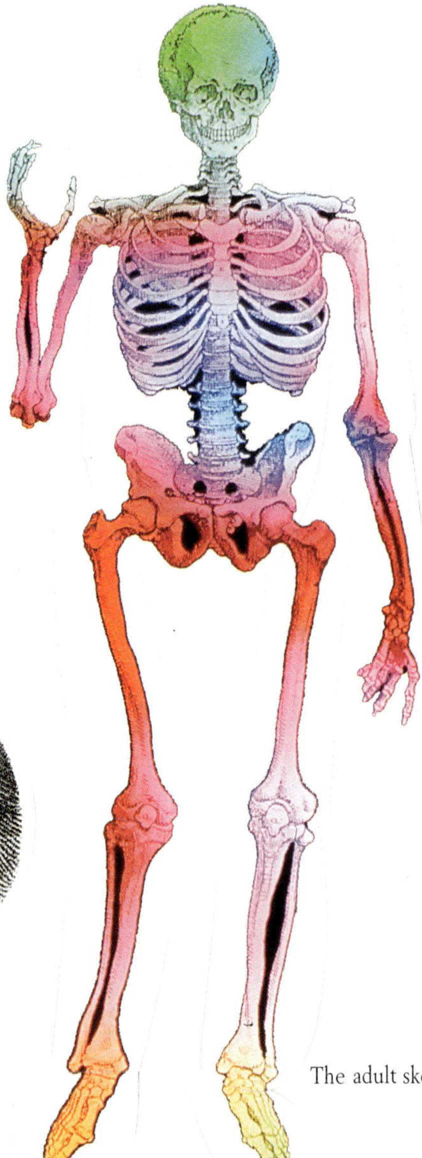

The adult skeleton

A fingerprint

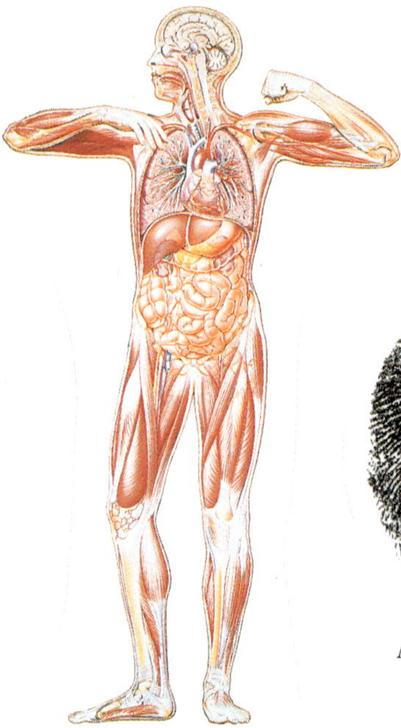

The organs of the body

Stickers

A six- week-old foetus

A three-month-old baby

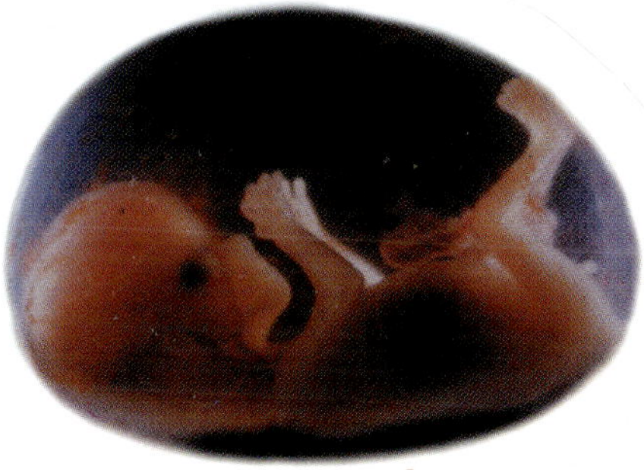

A four-month-old foetus

A six-month-old baby

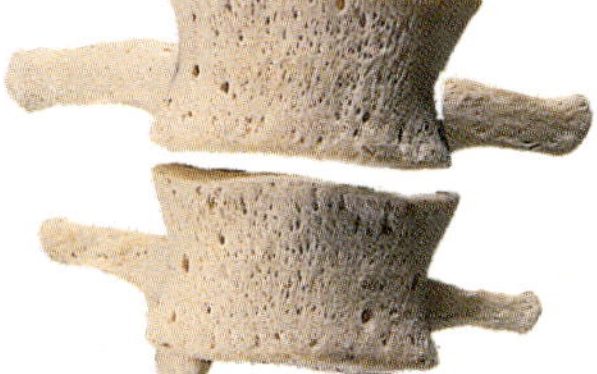

Short bones: two vertebrae

A long bone: the humerus

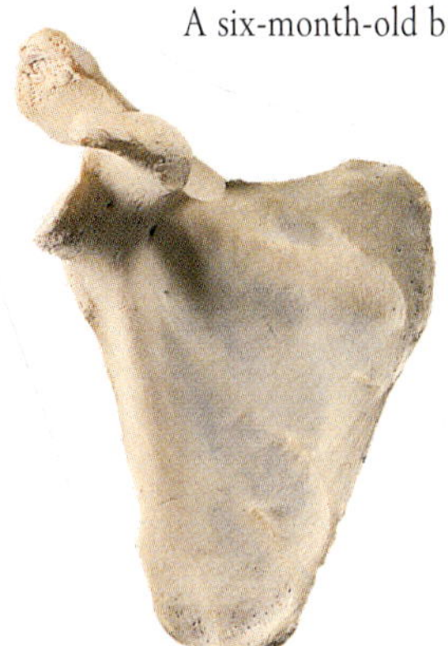

A flat bone: the shoulder blade

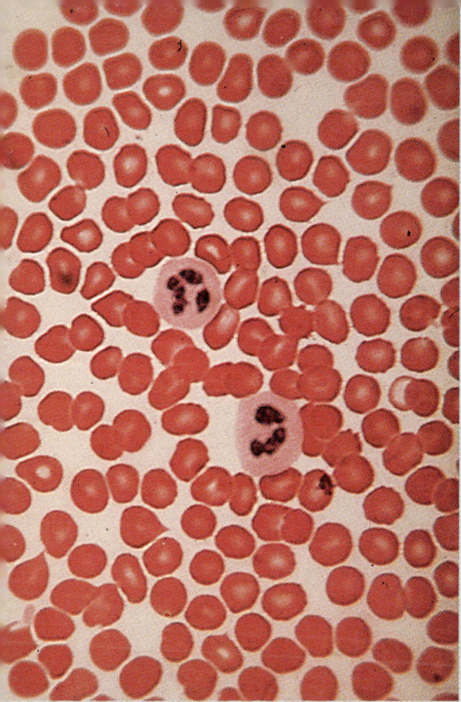
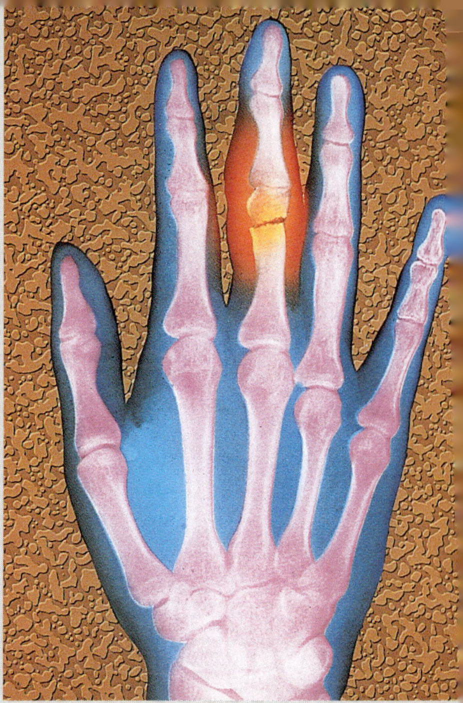
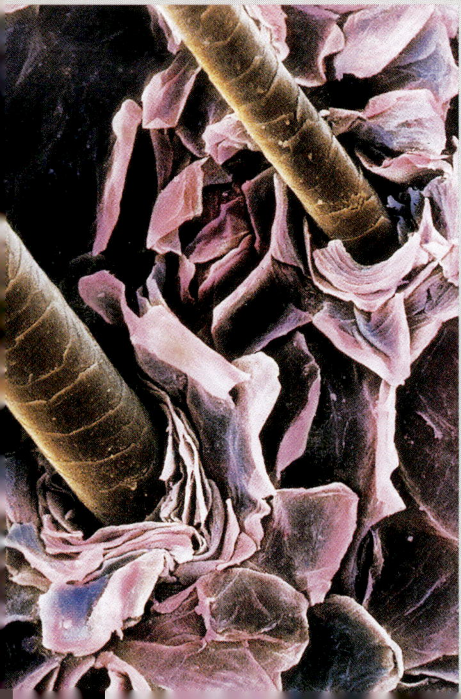

Postcard

Fractures

A fracture can be seen in an X-ray photograph. The broken bone may be encased in plaster or supported by a splint until it has healed.

postcard

Red blood cells

Red blood cells carry oxygen to all the cells in your body. They destroy any microbes that get into the blood. In the centre of the picture are two white blood cells.

Postcard

Pulling out teeth

In the old days, having a tooth pulled out was a dreadful experience. There was no anaesthetic to deaden the pain!

Postcard

Hairs

Hairs are made from a substance called keratin. They grow by forming new cells at the base of the root.

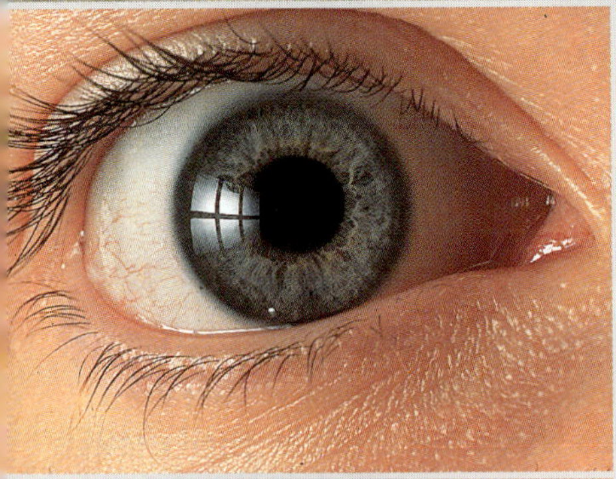

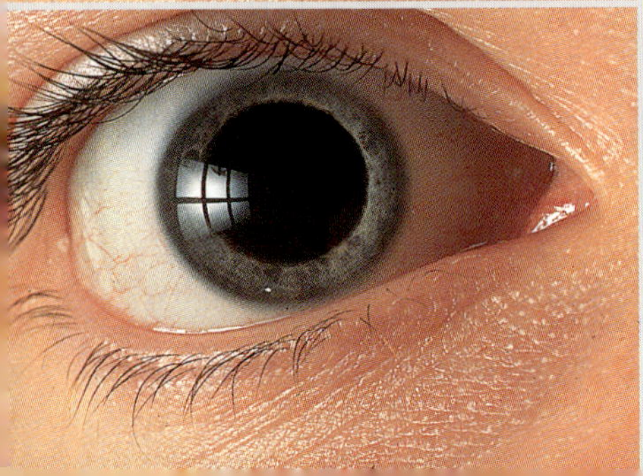

50

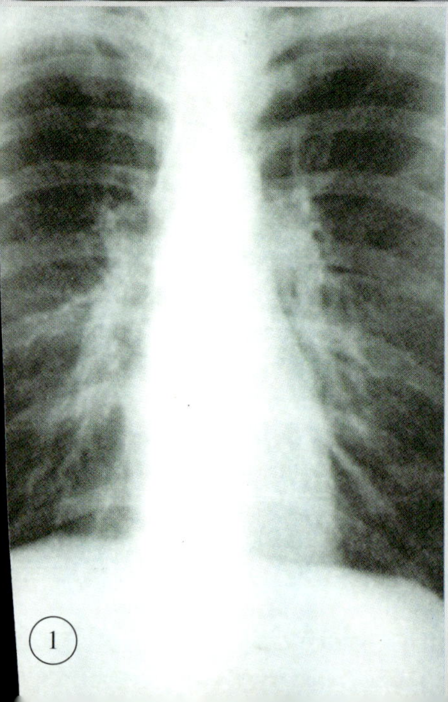

1

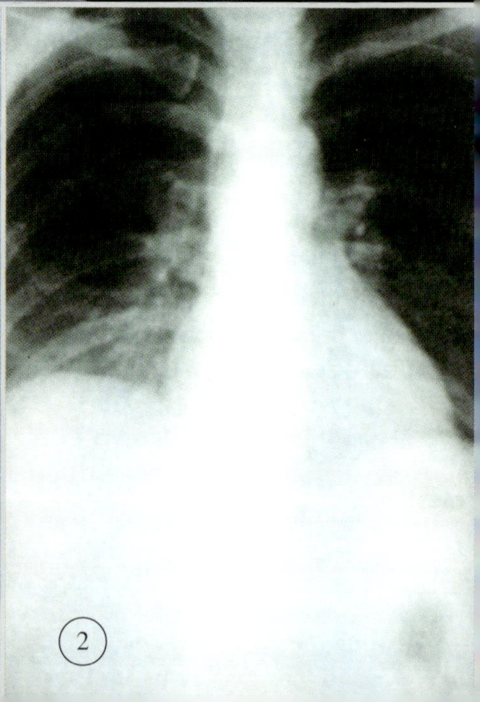

2

Postcard

A six-month-old foetus

At six months, an unborn baby measures 31 cm and weighs 1 kg.
It sleeps between 16 and 20 hours each day,
moves about more and more, and often has hiccups.

Postcard

Children of the world

Human beings vary in height, size, and colour of
their hair, eyes and skin.
But we are all made in the same way.

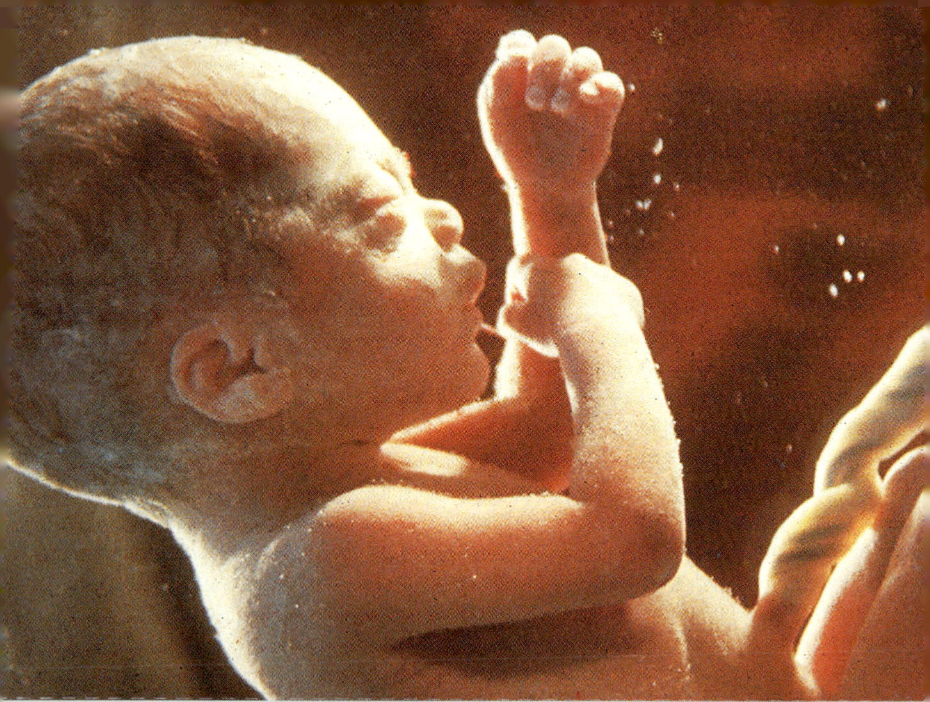